SY 0109192 1

D0727631

THE Business Ethics Activity Book

50 Exercises for Promoting Integrity at Work

ST.MARY'S UNIVERSITY COLLEGE

Marlene Caroselli, Ed.D.

AMACOM
American Management Association
New York • Atlanta • Brussels • Chicago • Mexico City
San Francisco • Shanghai • Tokyo • Toronto • Washington, D. C.

This publication is designed to provide accurate and authoritative information in regard to the subject matter covered. It is sold with the understanding that the publisher is not engaged in rendering legal, accounting, or other professional service. If legal advice or other expert assistance is required, the services of a competent professional person should be sought.

Library of Congress Cataloging-in-Publication Data

Caroselli, Marlene.
    The business ethics activity book : 50 exercises for promoting integrity at work / by Marlene Caroselli.
       p.   cm.
    Includes bibliographical references and indexes.
    ISBN 0-8144-7200-1
    1. Business ethics.   2. Leadership—Moral and ethical aspects.   I. Title.

HF5387.C347   2003
174′4—dc21

               2003005477

Printing number

10 9 8 7 6 5 4 3 2 1

Contents

PART A.	Ethical Leadership

1. **Intelligent Life in the Universe** 20
   This 30-minute exercise begins with a cartoon-prompt
   and proceeds to explore evidence of ethical behavior.

2. **You're Better Ough** 27
   A lexical challenge in this 30-minute exercise encourages ethical leaders
   to consider multiple viewpoints.

3. **Take Offense and Take the Offensive** 33
   Real-world scenarios are used in this exercise, which urges participants to
   speak up in order to right wrongs. It takes about 25 minutes to complete.

4. **Discerning Common Attributes** 38
   In this 20-minute exercise, participants identify attributes of ethical leaders
   and then engage in a related brain teaser.

5. **False Prophets** 43
   This 15-minute exercise examines the ethical responsibilities leaders have
   to weigh their words carefully before expressing them.

6. **Park Your Ethicar in the Harvard Yard** 47
   Participants in this 45-minute exercise compare current reasons for unethical
   behavior to those given in a Harvard study a quarter-century ago.

7. **You Don't Need Leaders to Tell People the Good News** 51
   This exercise, which requires 45 minutes, has participants complete a
   comparison matrix and then work on delivering a bad-news message.

8. **Machiavellian, Manipulative, or Masterful?** 56
   A quiz starts off this 30-minute exercise, after which participants explore
   two case studies taken from actual corporate occurrences.

PART B.   Ethical Workplace Conduct

PART C. Ethical Salesmanship

PART D.	# Ethical Management

PART E.	**Ethical Teamwork**

List of Handouts

Files in PDF format of the handouts in *The Business Ethics Activity Book* are also available online at www.amacombooks.org/businessethics.

Introduction

Almost every day we see the startling headlines: "Thousands lose retirement funds in collapse of company." "Accounting firm shreds documents." "Top executive commits suicide as investigation widens." "President pardons tax evader." "Police officer admits taking bribe." "Priest confesses to murder." "Crematory operator faces 339 charges of theft by deception." "Quality of surgical facilities woefully inadequate." "Conflicts cloud objectivity of corporate boards." "Directors' conflicts of interest often buried deep in firms' SEC filings." "Buffett tells directors to really dog auditors."

Tyco, Enron, Adelphia, WorldCom, Arthur Andersen, Merrill Lynch, ImClone Systems, Global Crossing—the deeds and misdeeds of corporate officers have entered the shame-filled, scandal-filled pages that capture for history unethical misappropriations and mis-reporting of funds. In the wake of these business meltdowns, change is finally underway. Corporate governance policies are being revisited, as are the methods corporations use to compensate their top executives. (Witness former CEO Jack Welch's decision to return his post-retirement perks to General Electric.) Many companies are contemplating, if not enforcing, the disclosure of executive stock plans and the treatment of stock options as expenses. (In the words of Warren Buffett, "The ratcheting up of compensation has been obscene.")

So common has been the breach of ethics by individuals and organizations in which we have placed our collective trust that new language has evolved to express our dismay. "Institutional betrayal" is the phrase that denotes the ersoin of faith that we once placed, without question, in organizations such as police forces, schools, churches, and bureau-cratic organizations. As a nation, we are in the midst of an identity crisis, redefining the rules that once governed us individually and as a whole.

Demands for reform are being made by the media, community members, activists, investors, stakeholders, Congress, employees, and the public at large. In fact, a survey by Dale Carnegie Training reported in *HR Fact Finder* ("Would You Blow the Whistle?" August 2002, page 6), finds that 75% of business people surveyed would "blow the whistle" if they discovered unethical management practices in their company.

Reforms will continue because of public outcries, and Congressional investigations will continue. Securities laws are being overhauled; the New York Stock Exchange and the

American Stock Exchange have proposed changes for closer regulation of corporate governance policies. The division that once separated the soft world of ethics (often considered subjective) and the hard world of finance (considered objective and quantifiable) is closing. Corporate social responsibility (CSR) is a force behind this development, as systems are developed to make leaders accountable and to create a culture that fulfills its responsibilities. Activism and accountability are no longer strange bedfellows.

There are those who believe rules cannot make someone moral—a person is either ethical or not. To be sure, no course, book, or training activity can convert an unethical person into an ethical one. We believe that you cannot "teach ethics." Yet, living as we do in such paradoxical times, we also believe:

➤ People may be engaged in activities they don't realize are unethical or illegal.

➤ Discussion and thought can create a cognitive dissonance that may lead to an altered state of behavior.

➤ Serious events can prompt serious shifts in perspective and action alike.

➤ One person can serve as a powerful force to offset the inertia born of long-standing practices.

For these reasons, we've compiled a series of activities for you to use as a training program in and of itself. These activities can also be used as part of training you are already doing in the areas of general Leadership, Corporate Citizenship, Sales, Management, and Teamwork. The activities are designed to probe, push, prod, and remove the calcified plaque that may have accumulated over time through repeated thoughts and actions. The individual activities may not effect sudden ethical behavior. However, they just might create an environment in which existing practices and policies can be critically examined. It is hoped that in time, such examination will lead to an improved moral climate.

This is not a book to be used only by trainers, however. Anyone who serves in an official or unofficial position of leadership can employ these activities to stimulate thought and discussion regarding appropriate decisions/behaviors/words/actions. Supervisors can use the activities during staff meetings; team leaders can energize their process improvement meetings; managers can distribute excerpts such as the monograph to department members; executive decision-makers can take some of the activities into account as they engage in strategic planning; and editors of the organizational newsletter can use the quizzes as integrity-driven fillers for their publication.

OVERVIEW OF THE BOOK

The Business Ethics Activity Book: 50 Exercises for Promoting Integrity at Work is divided into five sections, each of which is introduced via an interview with a leading business ethicist. Among them are authors Nan DeMars, Laurie Haughey, and Kristen Arnold; consultant/coach Robin Wilson; and attorney Tom Mitrano. With their own unique perspectives, these contributors present both microcosmic and macrocosmic views of ethics at work. Excerpted, they can serve as thought provoking material for anyone and everyone in the organization interested in ethical issues.

Each of the five sections has 10 exercises designed to stimulate discussion and promote inquiry regarding business ethics. The activities focus on Leadership, Corporate Citizenship, Salesmanship, Management, and Teamwork. (Despite their placement in one section or another, many of these activities are "crossovers"—with just a little tweaking, you can adapt them to several other purposes.) Contributing to this collection is a wide range of trainers from a variety of disciplines and locations, including Europe, India, Canada, and a broad cross-section of the United States.

I. Activities to Promote Ethical Leadership

Is it possible to operate within the letter of the law and still do something questionable at best, unethical at worst? Many believe, for example, that President Clinton's pardon of billionaire Marc Rich represented just such a scenario. On the other hand, is it possible to break the law and be considered honorable for having done so? Perhaps even to earn recognition for having done so? Such was the case involving Dorie Miller, who was honored posthumously for having brought down enemy aircraft at Pearl Harbor. Dorie Miller was a black sailor who broke the law of the land when he used weaponry labeled "For Whites Only."

This section promotes leadership, the kind that takes courage, commitment, and moral rectitude.

II. Activities to Promote Ethical Workplace Conduct

Toynbee's Law of Progressive Simplifications states, "The measure of a civilization's growth and sustainable vitality lies in its ability to transfer increasing amounts of energy and attention from the material side of life to the educational, psychological, cultural, aesthetic, and spiritual side." It is this law that serves as the foundation for *The Business Ethics Activity Book*, for the root of all evil truly is money and, if not money, the need to acquire "more" than we have—more power, more favor, more material things that bespeak our power or wealth. This is as true on a personal level as it is on the organizational level. Think of some of the most scandalous ethical breaches in recent corporate history. Uncover the reason behind the ethical breach and you'll almost always find money or power at its core.

The activities in this section help participants examine their micromotivation and macromotivation. They'll have opportunities to think about the power of ethical persuasion, the pros and cons of charisma, and choices and their consequences.

III. Activities to Promote Ethical Salesmanship

Whether it's an entire corporation, a sales division or department within that corporation, a single office, or an individual salesperson, the questions regarding business ethics cannot be answered without having definitions to serve as guidelines. We'll explore a number of issues that warrant the distribution of written definitions, such as values, goals, policies, and the very relationships the corporate body has to its suppliers, shareholders, competitors, employees, and, of course, to its clients.

Participants will be engaged in this section in surveys, role-plays, and panel discussions.

IV. Activities to Promote Ethical Management

Ethical management involves, in part, the larger issues of being socially responsible. Even if your participants are not in the corporate echelon that decides what profits can be earmarked for charitable purposes, they can still consider issues such as energy conservation; creating a work culture free of "isms" such as ageism and sexism; environmental damage; diversity; and everyday issues involving honesty and integrity. Participants will be encouraged to do more than think, though: they'll be asked to undertake some grass-roots movements in support of these issues.

Small-group activities and self-assessments are included among the activities that explore situational ethics.

V. Activities to Promote Ethical Teamwork

"Truth, justice, and the American way" are some of the topics examined in this section, which explores both loyalty and divided loyalties that team members often have to face. In several exercises, participants will act as "paper judges," ruling on real-world, real-workplace cases. In so doing, they'll learn to avoid the mistakes others have made in work situations similar to their own. They'll also have an opportunity to compare their rulings with those of the court.

In addition to litigation scenarios, participants will engage in activities of a gamelike nature, but with a serious intent: to engender ethical behavior by team members.

OVERVIEW OF THE EXERCISES

These exercises are diverse: contributing authors vary in their backgrounds and locations. International trainers from the Netherlands, India, and Canada are represented, as are American trainers with a wide range of specialties and experience. In addition to exercises by the editor/author, others have been submitted by academic leaders and entrepreneurial consultants.

The exercises range in duration from 10 minutes to an hour and a half. Each begins with the **Timeframe,** followed by an **Overview** and **Purpose.** The ideal **Group Size** and the best **Room Arrangement,** which can impact the amount of activity participants engage in and the degree of creativity they offer, are noted next. In the instructional construct, the required **Materials** and a step-by-step **Method** for executing the activity are listed.

What makes the activities unique are the **Discussion** prompts, which enable the trainer to widen the exercise's application, if he or she chooses to do so. This widening can be effected by:

➤ Using the questions as a prelude to doing the exercise.

➤ Employing the questions as a means of debriefing the exercise.

➤ Assigning different questions to different groups and having each explore the answers and then share those answers with other groups or with the entire group.

➤ Forming a panel of volunteers who will respond to these questions from the "audience."

➤ Inviting outsiders in as guest speakers and guest responders to these questions.

➤ Having participants write answers that will later be used in the company newsletter or for posting on an intranet system.

➤ Forming a small group who will leave the room to discuss the questions and then report back their answers, in lieu of a facilitator-led discussion.

➤ Citing the words of French anthropologist Claude Levi-Strauss—"The wise man doesn't give the right answers. He poses the right questions"—and then asking subgroups to add to the questions listed.

➤ Assigning individual questions to individual participants to be explored. Their individual "explorations" could be written on flipchart paper and posted around the room. Other participants can circulate among the posted papers and add their own comments.

➤ A volunteer can take these individual, written responses and submit them to the organizational newsletter or perhaps post them on the organization's Web site or on the intranet.

➤ As a means of extending the instructional emphasis beyond the classroom, for example, participants can take the questions back to their co-workers and supervisors and use them to explore various ethical issues.

Similarly, the **Quotation** in each activity can be used in the following ways:

➤ Post the quotations around the room and encourage participants to view and discuss them during breaks.

➤ Ask table group leaders to select a favorite quote posted around the room and discuss it within their groups.

➤ Write a given quote on the flipchart (or put it on a transparency) and use it as a stimulus for discussion involving the entire class.

➤ Select two quotes that imply contradiction and call on two different participants to explain/substantiate the differing viewpoints.

➤ Ask table groups to share examples of their own experiences as they relate to various quotes.

➤ Compile the quotes and distribute the sheet to participants. Periodically during the training day, call on someone to share his or her favorite quote and the relevance it has for that person.

Scattered throughout the activities are **Variations,** alternative ways of presenting the material or expanding its applicability. Variations should be regarded as ways to bring variety to a given exercise. These optional exercises may be integrated into the activity or they may be entirely separate activities. They may even be ideas for inclusion in related training sessions. As a rule, though, these tangential suggestions will enable session leaders to deepen and lengthen the actual activity and/or its post-session execution.

The **Points of Interest** present relevant research and material that can easily be incorporated into the exercises. These interesting, tangential tidbits can be used in the following ways:

➤ Begin the exercise with a "grabber"—a point of interest that will hook the group's attention. From there, move to the planned introduction.

➤ Use the point of interest as an example of the topic under discussion.

➤ Encourage discussion by sharing the point of interest and eliciting additional/related points from the group.

➤ Use the point of interest as a handout with relevant questions. Distribute it to groups for further discussion.

➤ Invite an expert to expand/explore the point of interest in relation to ethical practices in which participants' organizations are currently engaged.

➤ Draw parallels from the point of interest to current headlines in the news.

OVERVIEW OF THE METHODOLOGIES

A deliberately wide array of methodologies is employed within these activities, in view of the facts that:

➤ Adults used to multitasking need to switch their attention and focus from one kind of activity to another every 15 or 20 minutes.

➤ Dry and prolonged lectures do not appeal to adult learners as much as interactive, hands-on exercises in which they can do more than merely listen.

➤ Because some view the training experience as fraught with danger, since their reputations and competence are on display, these exercises have success virtually built in. Some are done privately, such as the assessments. Others are done in groups. Group assignments lessen the "exposure" of any one participant. Also, many of the assignments have neither right nor wrong answers—merely ideas to be explored. (Group discussions, for example, encourage the exchange of ideas.) We do recommend the trainer begin the day with an encouragement to participate but with the acknowledgment that some may prefer not to and that preference will be respected.

➤ Each of us has a preferred learning modality. Some of the methodologies are designed for visual intake, others for auditory, and still others for tactile expression.

Coupled with traditional classroom alternatives—video, flipcharts, and overhead transparencies—these exercises will enhance the typical learner's ability to absorb and retain ideas.

You'll find considerable flexibility with these exercises. Some can be used as icebreakers; others as energizers; still others as media for transferring knowledge via the written word. Some are designed to be taken back to the workplace and shared with colleagues. Some are designed to develop awareness; some diagnose; some develop documents that can be used on the job; some work to establish an ethical congruence between what is right and what is being done; some stimulate discussion; and some are simply enjoyable excursions into the world of ideas. All, however, have this in common—they are easy to use *and* they have a solid instructional core from which an ethical power can be released.

Even though the collection is primarily designed with traditional workshop training in mind, its use is not limited to trainers. These exercises can also be used by team leaders, supervisors, managers, and employees at any level. In other words, anyone interested in promoting an ethical culture and/or assuming a leadership role in continuous improvement will find in these pages numerous ideas that, when implemented, will truly make a difference.

Participant Assignments

Dyads, triads, teams, and whole-group exercises are used to achieve various purposes. When the exercise calls for some type of revelation or personal experience, the dyad or other small-group formation is suggested. When role-plays or other exercises calling for an observer to note an interpersonal exchange are used, we suggest grouping in triads. When an exercise merits the attention of the full group, the method incorporates speaking to the class as a whole, throughout a given exercise or for any one part of it.

Quizzes

The element of surprise can be a powerful force in retaining new knowledge. Many of the quizzes are designed to both elucidate and educate. By juxtaposing what they knew pre-quiz to what they learned post-quiz, participants can more quickly appreciate the width of the knowledge gap. Other quizzes are simply designed to test the degree of retention or to determine the degree of comprehension. (We recommend you never ask any one participant how he or she scored on a given quiz. In addition, never ask for a show of hands related to scores at the lower end of the continuum.)

Handouts

These are designed to supplement the intent of the exercise and to reinforce the main points being made. Handouts are also employed when participants need to have a common understanding of a situation, on the basis of which they'll take further action. Many of these handouts are designed with "portability" in mind so that participants can take them back to the office and share them with colleagues. Files in PDF format of the handouts for the activities are available at www.amacombooks.org/businessethics.

Case Studies

Case studies, owing to their real-world nature, enable participants to correlate their own experiences to someone else's and to project possible outcomes. When the actual outcomes are compared to their projections, participants can learn through discussion and analysis how best to handle comparable situations if and when they occur in their own lives. There's a safety net associated with case studies—they reveal pitfalls without making participants take the actual steps into those pits. By studying how someone else did or should have handled a difficult situation, participants can derive benefit that can later be applied to their own personal and professional situations.

Buzz Groups/Small Groups

There's a definite "buzz" that emanates from a classroom filled with small groups working on the same assignment and probably approaching it from different perspectives. Trainers can optimize the excitement by establishing a few ground rules, among them the time element and the fact that groups should try to keep their voices down so that others can work more easily. Additional factors to be considered include the following:

SELECTION OF GROUP PARTICIPANTS To avoid having people who work together all day sit together all day in a training session, here are several possibilities for grouping (or regrouping):

➤ Match well known business titles with their authors. (In a group of 20 participants, you'd have 10 titles and 10 authors.)

➤ As participants enter, give each a different colored candy kiss. Then assemble groups based on their colors.

➤ Write the name of the course on three large sheets of heavy paper or cardboard—each sheet will have the course name. Divide each sheet into irregular puzzle pieces (seven or eight pieces for each puzzle if class size, for example, is 22). Cut the pieces for each sheet and put them in an envelope. Shake the pieces up and then distribute one to each participant who enters the door. Groups form on the basis of puzzle pieces that fit together.

SELECTION OF GROUP LEADER To avoid having the most vocal person always serve as the group leader or reporter (and to avoid having the recorder always be a woman "with neat handwriting"), rotate the assignment as follows:

➤ Issue directions such as: "The person with the longest hair will be the reporter this time."

➤ Make this request: "Raise your hands with one finger protruding . . . preferably the little finger. Now, as you lower your hands, let the finger point to the person at your table whom you wish to be your group leader."

➤ Ask participants to figure out who has been with the organization for the longest period of time. That person becomes the group recorder.

REPORTS Group after group delivering oral reports, all day long, can be soporific. Consider these alternatives:

➤ Appoint a roving reporter who will circulate among the groups, sitting in just long enough to gain a sense of their discussions. The reporter then gives a brief overview of each group's discussion, allowing limited input from the groups to update or amend any of the reporter's comments.

➤ Have each group prepare a one-paragraph report on flipchart paper. You will then read each of the posted paragraphs.

➤ Challenge the group spokespersons to submit their reports in a creative fashion: a rhyme, an alliterative phrase, or a rap song, for example.

Guided Discussions

These activities are predicated on monographs that participants read in class. (Ideally, these can be distributed prior to the class so that valuable class time need not be spent on the reading. The advance arrangement also prevents the "lag" that results from people reading at different rates.) Once the group has internalized the material, you'll discuss it with questions that have been prepared ahead of time.

Scripts

Scripts bring out the creativity in participants. They also provoke insights and help participants convert theory to practical applications. Scripts have a way of sharpening the distinctions between best-case and worst-case scenarios and provide an interesting alternative to direct discussions of a given point. (Note: Scripts need not always be enacted. Often, the mere exploration of ideas on paper is sufficient to illustrate the point.)

Role-Play

You'll find some participants naturally hesitant to engage in role-plays. It's important to overcome that reluctance, though, because role-plays have an instructional value provided by no other method. Reluctance is usually tied to tension—a tension that results when individuals think about being someone or something other than themselves. If unchecked, tension can stultify creativity and can even block the natural flow of ideas.

One simple and quick way to relieve tension is the Y-E-S technique. Have the entire group engage in a deep, satisfying, collective **Y**awn just prior to the role-plays. Then provide **E**ducation about the value of role-plays: they help participants prepare for real-world encounters, they illustrate significant points, and they can actually be fun. Also provide education regarding the specific parameters of the roles and of the exercise itself. Finally, provide a few moments of **S**ilence, during which participants can collect their thoughts (perhaps even jot down a few notes). Then . . . let the role-plays begin.

Assessments

If it weren't for training opportunities, some participants would never introspect. The training environment is ideal for encouraging participants to take time to consider questions with potentially far-reaching implications. The assessments provided as part of some exercises invite self- and organizational analysis.

Panels

An interesting variation on the theme of knowledge acquisition is the use of panels. Panels can be composed of "outsiders," who are invited to the training room to present their views on a given topic. Following these presentations, a question-and-answer session will bring effective closure to the event.

Panels can also be composed of participants—either volunteers or spokespersons selected by their table groups to present summaries of the work that the groups have just completed. Panel members, representing the class as a whole, can exchange ideas on behalf of their groups. (An alternative would be to have participants write additional questions for panel members and to have a moderator collect these and present them to the panel for response.)

Fishbowls

This technique involves having one group work in the center of the room while the remainder of the class sits in a wider circle around them, observing their interactions. It's quite effective, for example, for the inside group to participate in a team meeting while the outside group observes their interactions and their effectiveness in accomplishing a given task.

A FINAL NOTE

It would be remiss of us not to mention the ethical obligations you have as a trainer, especially a trainer of business ethics. At the risk of offending veteran trainers, but as an important checklist for new trainers, here is a list of responsibilities/recommendations that bespeak both professionalism and an ethical commitment to the profession. (Ideally, most of the following behaviors are already part of your professional persona.)

➤ I know this subject well enough to be considered something of an expert in it.

➤ I get to the room at least half an hour early to set it up and to greet early arrivals.

➤ I do all I can to make participants feel welcome, including the placement of a welcome sign on the door or the writing of the word on the flipchart.

➤ I begin with an introduction of the course and its purpose, of myself and my credentials for teaching the course, and then with introductions of the participants themselves.

➤ I present an overview or agenda of what the course entails.

➤ I make a sincere effort to remember names of the participants.

➤ I periodically review the material or provide summaries.

➤ I consciously avoid sarcasm, vulgarity, inappropriate humor, and references that may be offensive.

➤ I anticipate questions that will arise and prepare responses to them.

➤ I employ anecdotes to illustrate points.

➤ I assure participants they will never be made to feel uncomfortable.

➤ I never lecture for more than 15 minutes at a stretch.

➤ I incorporate humor into my presentation.

➤ I include relevant news events and statistics in my presentation.

➤ I am physical with knowledge—that is, make dramatic gestures from time to time.

➤ I provide a change of pace on a regular basis.

➤ I consciously think about ways to make the presentations interactive.

➤ I encourage participants to meet and work with others in the room.

➤ I invite feedback about the presentation.

➤ I strive to relate the material to participants' jobs and objectives.

➤ I attempt to learn as much as I can about participants and their organizations or departments.

➤ I schedule breaks as needed.

➤ I ensure the screen and flipchart can be seen by every participant.

➤ I keep abreast of developments in the field.

➤ I revise my materials on a continual basis.

➤ I provide professional-looking handouts and references.

➤ I employ a wide variety of methodologies.

➤ I invite questions and feedback on my presentation.

➤ I invite (but put limits on) the telling of "war stories."

➤ I make myself available to participants.

➤ I provide ways for participants to be continuous learners.

➤ I design effective closure.

Ethical Leadership

INTRODUCTION

Five Standards of Excellence Practiced by Ethical Leaders

LAURIE HAUGHEY

For quite some time, picking up *The Wall Street Journal* meant reading stories rife with indictments of CFOs, CEOs, and accountants. Though many leaders practice good principles, clearly it is time to inspect closely what it means to lead with ethics. The world is full of strong leaders; however, leadership is a neutral term. It can be good or bad. Stalin, Hitler, Mussolini, and Mao Tse Tung were regarded as good political leaders at some point in time by a certain element of the population. History has proven, however, that each was guilty of an immoral use of the tremendous power his leadership afforded him.

What will history tell us about our current leaders of industry? Are they leading their companies in an ethical way? Perhaps the best barometer of achievement in this regard is the sustainable success of an organization over the long haul. For when you whittle commerce down to the point of its raison d'être, you find its ethical basis. Is it not the mission and ethical imperative of every publicly held establishment to absorb the cost of doing business, produce a quality product for its customers, provide sustenance for its members, and turn a profit that can be reinvested to make the company stronger for lean times? One company has been doing this well for more than 120 years. General Electric's recent declining stock values may trouble investors, but it still was recognized as one of *Fortune*'s *2002 Global Most Admired Companies* and received the highest marks for its quality of management. Compare it to the relatively young MCI WorldCom, a company struggling in a quagmire of ethical issues, and the sustaining success of GE is clearly manifested.

The following chapter leads you through hands-on exercises that will cause you to reflect on the many elements that comprise ethical leadership. To get started, we will discuss the following five components of ethical leadership: communication, quality, collaboration, succession planning, and tenure.

Ethical Communication

Ethical leaders set the standard of truth for every employee they lead. The moment people take leadership positions, they have an opportunity to place the highest premium on truthfulness. Recent cases of fiscal malfeasance at Enron, WorldCom, and Arthur Andersen illustrate the need for every form of communication leaders put forth to be an accurate representation. Yet, leading by example cannot be the only process by which this standard is relayed. It must become a company slogan, from the accounting office to the shop floor, that "Truth is Job 1." Truthful information is quality information to the CEO, board of directors, and investors.

Jim Collins, a noted researcher on leadership, advises leaders to "conduct autopsies, without blame," and cites companies such as Philip Morris whose executives talked openly about the "7-UP disaster."[1] Even when statistical evidence does not reflect well on a division or the financial status of the entire company, a plan of action to thwart disaster may be implemented and several lessons learned through open communication to ensure the sustainability of the organization.

Ethical Quality

An ethical leader understands that three factors ensure the global market competitiveness of an organization: a quality product, quality customer service, and quality delivery. Leaders must champion the processes of quality throughout the organization, benchmarking successful organizations, incorporating innovations in quality, and setting standards and measurements in every department. Leaders have several tools to ensure quality. They don't have to be Master Black Belts in Six Sigma or understand all the intricacies of lean manufacturing or supply chain management to see how each improves quality. They are sold on the merits of having a quality. They know that cutting waste translates to saving time and money for the organization. It is the leader's responsibility to drive, steer, and fund the quality initiative throughout the organization. For only when top leaders fully endorse a quality initiative does it have a chance of becoming fully implemented and the harvest days of savings can occur.

Bob Galvin, Chairman of Motorola, implemented Six Sigma throughout the company in the early 1980s. Just two years after "launching Six Sigma, Motorola was honored with the Malcolm Baldrige National Quality Award."[2] Even the federal government is investigating the merits of this management tool. Several local government agencies are already using Six Sigma, and the federal government may employ Six Sigma in its war on terrorism. With a failure rate of 3.4 per million products/actions or 99.99966% accuracy, agencies would be better informed and lives could be saved if only one of "every 294,000 vital pieces of information . . . [was] . . . erroneously discarded."[3]

Ethical Collaboration

Ethical leaders need many advisors. They pick the most astute within their organizations and hire some from other companies, but they surround themselves with answers. Wise leaders collaborate to incorporate best practices, solve problems, and address the issues facing their organizations. Regrettably, the natural tendency of leaders is to draw in a close, and more often than not, closed circle of advisors. Unfortunately, the smaller the group, the less the prospect of collectively providing the leader advice on the full range of

---

[1]Collins, Jim. *Good to Great: Why Some Companies Make the Leap and Others Don't*, p. 77.
[2]Pande, et al. *The Six Sigma Way: How GE, Motorola, and Other Top Companies Are Honing Their Performance*, p. 7.
[3]*USA Today,* October 31, 2002, p. 5B.

issues facing the organization. But the leader who collaborates ethically makes better decisions for the organization. How is that possible? Leaders who use ethical collaboration keep their circle of advisors more open and fluid. The objective of the ethical leader is to reduce the risks taken by the organization by assigning trustworthy experts/advisors to every situation—from R&D decisions to customer-driven needs. Advisors' findings determine decisions of the leader who becomes better equipped to make judgments based on two critical elements: more feasible solutions and viable processes needed to exact the solutions.

Many states suffer the woes of underfunded education. Recently, South Carolina imposed a 15% budget cut, with more cuts promised in the future. The President of Clemson University, Jim Barker, pulled in campus-wide experts in their fields to provide solutions. Robert McCormick, an internationally known economist, among others, was assigned the task of creating a fiscal roadmap to ensure Clemson would sustain itself through time. While his advisors provided him with sound solutions, Barker remained focused on the overall mission of the university and its drive to become a top-20 public university. Ethical collaboration serves another important role, however. As Barker maintains an open and fluid circle of advisors while assigning the right people to the variety of issues facing the institution, he serves to broaden his and others' awareness of promising internal successors.

Ethical Succession Planning

If principled leaders possess a need for control, they satisfy that need by establishing strong organizational standards and operational procedures for quality and communication. Yet for the long-term success of the organization, ethical leaders must set aside issues of "turf" and let other leaders surface within the company, giving potential successors opportunities to exercise and build their leadership skills. Once identified, these few should be personally mentored by the leader, given opportunities for 360° communications, and trained for the roles they may one day assume.

In his book, *Good to Great: Why Some Companies Make the Leap . . . and Others Don't*, Jim Collins identifies Chrysler with many organizations that achieve greatness only to have it slip away through time. While examining the long list of organizations in his study, Collins notes that under Lee Iacocca Chrysler followed "a pattern . . . found in every unsustained comparison: a spectacular rise under a tyrannical disciplinarian, followed by an equally spectacular decline when the disciplinarian stepped away, leaving behind no enduring culture of discipline . . ."[4] Arguably Chrysler faltered without Iacocca at the helm because he had failed to practice ethical collaboration to the point that a succession plan was devised.

Ethical Tenure

How long should a leader lead? Whereas the most important leader in the American government leads for 4 to 8 years, industry has no governing standard to length of tenure.

---

[4]Collins, Jim. *Good to Great: Why Some Companies Make the Leap . . . and Others Don't*, p. 133.

Should leadership in industry, like its counterpart in government, have a shelf life? The answer lies on the conduct of the leader. Leadership expert Peter Block contends that "We search, so often in vain, to find leaders we can have faith in."[5] Further, he notes that leadership is more often rated on the trustworthiness of the individual than on his or her particular talents, and that the mission of the ethical leader is to serve the institution and not themselves.[6] Jim Collins identifies this category of executives as Level 5 Leaders: leaders who are able to "channel their ego needs away from themselves and into the larger goal of building a great company."[7]

Ethical leaders collaborate and provide their organizations succession plans that ensure the growth of the organization over time. They feel that they lead at the request of the company, customers, board of directors, and stockholders. If each of these entities' trust in the leader remains unchallenged, the leader should lead until he or she chooses to step down. However, whereas even the best of leaders turn the company over to a new set of watchful eyes eventually, the leader who is irreparably jeopardizing the sacred trust of employees, customers, and the public at large should step aside and let a better leader take the helm.

Conclusion

Much has been written about leadership. Regrettably, less time and thought has been afforded the concept of ethical leadership. Perhaps it is the very lack of discussion about what it means to lead with ethics that has created the current business environment of SEC investigations into improprieties, dot-com greed, and the general public's lack of faith in the stock market. Though we would have preferred that the government did not have to force the issue of business propriety through threats and legislation, apparently for some leaders fear and not moral certitude is their personal motivator. As we look to the future however, perhaps dialogues such as the many presented in this book will be remembered in the critical decision-making of our next generation of leaders.

Works Cited

Block, Peter. Stewardship: *Choosing Service Over Self-Interest.* San Francisco: Berrett-Koehler Publishers, Inc., 1993.

Collins, Jim. *Good to Great: Why Some Companies Make the Leap . . . and Others Don't.* New York: HarperCollins Publishers, Inc., 2001.

"Feds may unleash Six Sigma on terrorism." *USA Today,* October 31, 2002, p. 5B

Pande, Peter S., Robert P. Neuman and Roland R. Cavanagh. *The Six Sigma Way: How GE, Motorola, and Other Top Companies Are Honing Their Performance.* New York: McGraw-Hill Companies, Inc., 2000.

---

[5]Block, Peter. *Stewardship: Choosing Service Over Self Interest,* p. 9.
[6]Ibid.
[7]Collins, Jim. *Good to Great: Why Some Companies Make the Leap and Others Don't,* p. 21.

LAURIE HAUGHEY is the author *of Athletes Off the Field: A Model for Team Building and Leadership Development Through Service Learning.* Employed by Clemson University since 1989, she serves as Conference Organizer/Training Development Director in the university's Department of Off-Campus, Distance, and Continuing Education. Laurie, a former track and field student athlete, earned degrees in English and sociology from Clemson. She has dedicated her career—in academics and earlier in athletics—to promoting lifelong learning and collaborative endeavors that serve to build each participant's leadership experience. While working in athletics as an academic advisor, Laurie initiated a peer leadership group among the football student athletes. Leaders In Football and Education, a.k.a. LIFE LINE, completes 10 service learning projects each year and works in partnership with elementary schools and other service-missioned charity groups. Laurie is the former president of Clemson's Letterman's Association.

ETHICAL LEADERSHIP

1 Intelligent Life in the Universe

Approximately 30 minutes

Purpose

To prompt discussion about the need for leaders to provide evidence of an ethical foundation on which their platforms are constructed.

Group Size

Any number of individuals can participate, ideally divided into groups of four or five.

Room Arrangement

If possible, provide tables accomodating four or five participants each.

Materials

➤ Projector for transparencies or for PowerPoint slides

➤ Transparency 1.1, *"The Surest Sign"*

➤ Transparency 1.2, *"The Surest Sign"*

➤ Transparency 1.3, *"Sure Signs of Ethical Leadership"*

➤ Transparency 1.4, *"My Own Ethical Leadership"*

Procedure

1. Begin by asking how many read the cartoon strip "Calvin and Hobbes." (**Note:** If possible, cut out several "Calvin and Hobbes" cartoons from the newspaper or a book and distribute one to each table. Allow a few minutes for the cartoon to be read.)

2. State that the cartoon's originator, Bill Watterson, has a line that you find amusing. Put Transparency 1.1 on the projector for transparencies or for PowerPoint slides and read aloud:

"The surest sign that intelligent life exists elsewhere in the universe is. . ."

3. Ask groups to come up with two or three completions for this sentence opening. Allow no more than 5 minutes for the assignment.

4. Have a spokesperson from each group share the group's favorite line.

5. Next, show Transparency 1.2 revealing Bill Watterson's punch line: "that it has never tried to contact us!"

6. Show Transparency 1.3 and ask small groups to decide on a leader whose actions they can analyze. This could be an organizational leader in their own firm or a different organization; it could be a state leader, a national leader, or an international leader. Once they've determined what leader to consider, have them find three specific attributes they believe manifest ethical behavior in that leader. This portion of the exercise will take about 10 minutes.

7. Ask a spokesperson from each group to make a brief presentation regarding the leader who was selected and the ethical behaviors exhibited by that person.

8. Have participants work alone to complete Transparency 1.4, which asks them to think about ways they demonstrate adherence to ethical standards.

9. Finally, ask them to work in pairs or triads to discuss their thoughts.

Variation

Ask for volunteers to write an article for a management publication (or their own organizational newsletters) based on the vitally important connections between leadership and ethical behavior.

In courses dealing with conflicts in the workplace, the trainer is bound to cite the need for developing and maintaining mutual respect. That respect is often dependent on ethical behaviors; the erosion of that respect and of trust is often related to the absence of ethical behaviors or—worse yet—the manifestation of *un*ethical behaviors.

Discussion

➤ Is it ethical for a leader deliberately to find ways to demonstrate his or her ethics?

➤ Is it possible for a given action to be viewed as both ethical and unethical by two different people or groups? If so, what examples can you think of?

➤ Is there a danger for a leader who makes his or her intents and intentions known?

Quotation

"I have learnt silence from the talkative, toleration from the intolerant, and kindness from the unkind; yet strange, I am ungrateful to these teachers."
—Kahlil Gibran

Points of Interest

One of the most flagrant examples of unethical behavior is the violation of federal copyright laws. Duplicating software violates Section 17 of that law. Advise others that the only legal reason for copying a program is for an individual's reliance on a backup disk. Individuals who break this law could be fined $25,000, imprisoned, or both.

THE SUREST SIGN

"The surest sign
that intelligent life
exists elsewhere in
the universe is. . .

THE SUREST SIGN

"The surest sign
that intelligent life
exists elsewhere
in the universe is. . .

that it has never
tried to contact us!"

—Cartoonist Bill Watterson ("Calvin & Hobbes")

SURE SIGNS OF ETHICAL LEADERSHIP

"Sure signs that

_____
(person's name)

of _____
(organization)

exhibits ethical leadership are:

1) _____ ,
2) _____ ,
3) _____ .

MY OWN ETHICAL LEADERSHIP

"The surest signs that my own leadership is ethical include

_____,

_____;

and

_____.

ETHICAL LEADERSHIP

You're Better Ough

Approximately 30 minutes

Overview

The numerous pronunciations of the *"ough"* syllable (including the sound of "off," as in "You're better off") form the basis of this exercise, which encourages leaders to consider the multiple perspectives from which their actions may be viewed.

Purpose

To develop the essential leadership ability that involves considering several viewpoints that could be applied to a given situation. Just as 360° perspectives are considered critical to the success of organizational leaders and managers, this microcosmic example encourages the consideration of multiple viewpoints, thus diminishing the likelihood of groupthink.

Group Size

Any number of individuals can participate. Participants will first work in triads and then in groups of six. A spokesperson from each group will participate in a panel discussion.

Room Arrangement

If possible, provide flexible seating so that triads can be formed; later, seats can be arranged for an audience to face a panel of presenters.

Materials

➤ Flipchart and marking pens
➤ Projector for transparencies or for PowerPoint slides
➤ Transparency 2.1, *"You're Better Ough"*
➤ Handout 2.1, *"Two Sides to Every Story"*

Procedure

1. Begin with a brain teaser for participants, who are seated in triads: How many words can they think of that contain different pronunciations of the combined letters "ough"? Call on a spokesperson from each group to share the words they've thought of.

2. Write the words on a flipchart, noting that a given combination of letters is subject to numerous possible pronunciations, depending on the words selected.

3. Show the transparency and compare the pronunciations with those on the flipchart to determine which may have been omitted from the flipchart list.

4. Segue from the brain teaser to the fact that a leader's actions can be viewed from various points along a wide spectrum of possibilities. Discuss the fact that perception is stronger than truth. While a leader may believe he or she is displaying ethical behavior and may actually be doing so, if that behavior is viewed as unethical, the perception will take precedence over the truth. The best communicators consider various viewpoints and find the common truth that runs through all of them. Ask for real-life instances of two people holding opposing points of view with each having truth (or a portion of it) on his or her side. Ethical leaders take time to explore these differing viewpoints and again, to find the compromise positions within them.

5. Distribute the handout, "Two Sides to Every Story," and ask triads to join another triad to form a team of six. The team will discuss the questions presented on the handout.

6. Have a spokesperson from each team come forward to sit at a table. The individuals on this panel will present the viewpoints held by their team. You will moderate and shall invite questions from the audience.

7. Next, announce the actual judgment in a similar situation: the United States Supreme Court (Mullins v. Pfizer Inc.) sided with the employee. The court ruled that, having announced an early retirement package and then denying the benefits to retiring employees, the company had treated employees unfairly. The company was found to have misrepresented its intentions.

If you, as an ethical leader, wish to act fairly and to avoid the appearance of impropriety, keep these points in mind:

➤ Make no advance announcements. Wait until your policy has been clearly defined.

➤ If possible, have an attorney review the policy to ensure there is no ethical or legal breach.

➤ Avoid using phrases such as "seriously considering" that may hold false promise for employees.

➤ Meet face-to-face with employees to lay out the final policy and to answer questions they have.

➤ Form a rumor-quashing committee to dispel possible misunderstandings.

➤ Issue policy reminders and policy restatements several different times in several different ways.

➤ If your organization does not have specific policies in effect for various HR issues, assume a leadership position and begin to codify the consequences of changes so that fair and ethical treatment will ensue.

8. Conclude by noting that the speed element governing business today leads to rapid-fire decisions. Corporate values are shifting, as are streamlining efforts. In the process, traditionally held beliefs and assumptions are changing. And, just as five different people could pronounce "ough" in five different ways, corporate changes that are not clearly spelled out can be interpreted in numerous ways. Ethical leadership involves communication that leaves no room for "wiggling"— for either side.

Variation

Try this experiment with the group to illustrate how the same event can elicit different accounts from various individuals, each of whom is probably certain that his or her version is the accurate one. Plan to have a colleague who is not familiar to the class participants enter the room and ask for the flipchart (or overhead projector or some other common object). You will pretend not to know this individual and will politely protest, stating that you had arranged for the equipment and need it to present your program. The colleague will become more belligerent and insistent and will finally just pick up your equipment and take it out of the room with a few choice words and a loud slam of the door. Express your shock to the group and enlist their help: say that you intend to report the incident and have them describe exactly what happened. Collect the reports and have a volunteer analyze them for similarities and differences.

Discussion

➤ Have you ever argued with someone who saw the same thing you saw (or heard the same thing you heard) and yet had an entirely different interpretation of the event? If so, recall the details.

➤ What advantages can you cite when a multiplicity of viewpoints surround a given event? What disadvantages?

➤ How can a leader best make use of the diversity of thought associated with his or her cause or proposal?

Quotation

"Before you speak, listen. Before you write, think. Before you spend, earn. Before you invest, investigate. Before you criticize, wait. Before you pray, forgive. Before you quit, try. Before you retire, save. Before you die, give."
—William A. Ward

Points of Interest

Note that typically a casual remark cannot be regarded as the equivalent of terms in an employment contract. However, this situation contained more than a casual remark. The setting was formal, the prompt was a specific question asked by the employee, and a promise was made—more than once, in fact. In the actual case, the promise was made in front of a witness, further weakening the company's position.

YOU'RE BETTER OUGH

A ploughman with a face like dough and hands rough as sandpaper, thoughtfully listened to the song "Scarborough Fair." Soon, though, he slipped into a slough of reverie, in which he coughed, hiccoughed, and then fell gently asleep.

Two Sides to Every Story

SITUATION

Susan Atkins worked on the assembly line at an automotive parts factory. Although she occasionally found the job tedious, she liked it nonetheless, especially the benefits and good wages guaranteed by her union contract. One day her boss of 12 years, Anthony Trotto, called her in and said he was planning to reclassify her job to one that was not covered by the contract. In the next few weeks, Susan met several times with Mr. Trotto and each time asked about job security. She was repeatedly assured that her job was secure and as long as she continued to work well, she wouldn't have a problem. Unfortunately, Susan's performance evaluations began moving toward the "unacceptable" range and she was ultimately fired.

QUESTIONS

1. If you had been Susan, would you have sued?
2. If so, on what grounds?
3. If you were the automotive company, what would your defense have been?
4. Can an oral assurance be considered a contract?
5. If so, what assurances have you made lately?
6. How would they hold up in court?
7. How do you think the court would rule in such cases?

Take Offense and Take the Offensive

Approximately 25 minutes

Overview

Ethical leaders have a finely developed sense of justice. They take offense when it is warranted and then proactively take steps to ensure offensive actions are not repeated. This exercise uses real-world scenarios to stimulate discussion regarding those types of actions.

Purpose

➤ To heighten participants' awareness of inappropriate behavior.

➤ To caution against the use of certain negative-impact words.

➤ To stimulate thought regarding appropriate actions to be taken as a result of inappropriate behavior.

Group Size

Any number of individuals can participate. Participants will first work alone and then in pairs. The exercise concludes with a full-group discussion.

Room Arrangement

No special arrangements are required.

Materials

Handout 3.1, *"Your Reaction/Your Reply?"*

Procedure

1. Distribute the handout and begin this exercise by pointing out that certain words are obviously offensive to different groups. Surprisingly, though, not every person within a given group finds a given word offensive. Some women, for example, don't mind being referred to as "girls"; others take immediate

umbrage. Still, it's best to avoid those words and phrases that are well recognized as insulting.

2. Point out that it's the leader's ethical responsibility to create a workplace environment that is free from prejudice of any kind. Employees have a right not to be disparaged, mocked, insulted, threatened, or offended.

3. Next, explain that sometimes we employ an expression without realizing that it might sound prejudicial or insulting. The handout explores four actual incidents. Participants should read about the four incidents and then share their thoughts with a partner.

4. Transition next to references based on current events (President Bush's declaration of the war against terrorism as a "crusade," for example) or to examples elicited from participants regarding similar incidents.

5. Conclude the exercise by leading a discussion (and, ideally, recording the results) that explores things an organizational leader/manager can and should do to ensure employees are treated respectfully.

Variation
_____

This exercise can be easily adapted for programs emphasizing cultural diversity, conflict in the workplace, leadership, and communication skills.

Discussion
_____

➤ What, specifically, can a leader do to ensure offensive remarks are kept out of the workplace?

➤ What is the downside of being too politically correct?

➤ Can you think of instances in which a national figure was criticized/chastised for making seemingly innocent remarks?

➤ If you, in all innocence, had made such a remark, would you feel compelled to apologize for it?

➤ How do First Amendment rights impinge on remarks that might cause offense?

Quotation
_____

"The best effect of fine persons is felt after we have left their presence."
—Ralph Waldo Emerson

**Points
of Interest**

In the case of *Dan Antoni vs. Employment Security Department
of the State of Washington,* No. 15764-4-III, the court ruled that
Bonnie Showalter, who had been fired for being rude to
customers, was entitled to benefits denied her when she was
terminated. The court agreed the behavior was inappropriate
but that it did not constitute misconduct—even though her boss
had been told he would lose his licensing subagency if such
behavior continued. Ms. Showalter claimed a strict diet caused
her to "veer out of control." This claim ran counter to the
definition of misconduct, which means a "willful act."

There's the letter of the law and the spirit of the law. Even
though employees may be within their rights to act as they do,
you may wish to encourage them to abide by higher standards,
standards that include treating others respectfully. According to
the *IRS Employment Review,* released April 2, 2002, bullying,
harassment, and rudeness top the list of workplace complaints.
Rudeness may not be illegal, but it doesn't fit into the commonly
held views of what constitutes ethical, respectful leadership.

Your Reaction/ Your Reply?

DIRECTIONS

Decide what, if anything, you would have said or done if you had been the person toward whom the offensive, perhaps innocently offensive, remark was directed. Be prepared to explain the rationale behind your decision to say/do something or nothing.

SITUATION 1

Jeannette Guzman was engaged in a discussion of multitasking consulting at the annual office party. She excused herself at one point and headed to the hors d'oeuvres table, where she was approached by another employee who "complimented" her with these words: *"Jeannette, I just have to tell you how much I enjoyed listening to you just now. You are so intelligent for a Mexican."*

SITUATION 2

Donna Silverstein was having a birthday lunch with four co-workers, when one of them admired her handbag, asking where she had purchased it. Donna recalled that she had purchased it when she was in Morocco, at an outdoor casbah. *"Oh,"* the other woman asked, clearly interested, *"Haggling is such fun. Did you have to jew down the merchant to get it?"*

SITUATION 3

It's the first day on the job for Chynna Kim. One of her fellow workers, in an effort to welcome her, walks up, extends his hand, and jovially observes: *"I see they've hired another Chink."*

SITUATION 4

Linda Karolla (nee Giordano) has just transferred to a new department. The other secretaries took her to lunch to help orient her to the department. One of them cautions her: *"Mr. Martiello heads Accounting and he's very, very careful about how money is spent. (His nickname is 'Tightwad.') He would never actually gyp anyone out of their money, but he always tries to cut expensive corners. So be careful, Linda. If you overspend, he just might call in the Mafia!"*

ETHICAL LEADERSHIP

Discerning Common Attributes

Approximately 20 minutes

Overview

This brain teaser encourages critical thinking about the attributes shared by ethical leaders who stand on a common ground of correctness. Participants first identify such attributes and then engage in a mental challenge designed to elicit critical thinking in general terms.

Objectives

To generate insight and discussion regarding the attributes of ethical leaders.

Group Size

Any number of participants can engage in this exercise.

Room Arrangement

No special arrangements are required.

Materials

➤ Flipchart and marking pens

➤ Handout 4.1, *"Standing on Common Ground"*

➤ Optional: Provide token prizes for the winning pair, such as a paperback book about critical thinking or perhaps crossword puzzles from the daily newspaper.

Procedures

1. Ask participants to think about the most ethical leader they have ever known either personally or by reputation. Elicit examples from the group and write the names of the ethical leaders cited on the flipchart.

2. Then ask them to think about the specific attributes (mention "critical thinking" in particular as an example) that these individuals displayed or specific actions they took. List these on the flipchart as participants share them.

3. Have participants choose a partner and ask each person to select one attribute or action from the flipchart list and explain how he or she would incorporate it into his or her leadership style or circumstances.

4. Distribute the handout and ask the pairs to analyze the statements related to ethical leadership. (Optional: Announce that the first pair with the highest number of correct answers will win a prize.) The answers are 1ab; 2c; 3bc; 4a; 5abcd. Compliment the pair who found them fastest.

5. Conclude with a brief discussion relating critical-thinking skills to leadership, particularly the skills of discerning emerging patterns, making tough decisions, and being fair to all parties concerned. Relate this leadership skill to current events, if possible.

Note that effective leaders go beyond the givens, move into the unknown, and refuse to cling to the prevalent logic as they pursue ethical outcomes. Have the group consider the insistence of Chief Charles Moose of Montgomery County that the public not depend exclusively on the FBI profile (which ultimately proved to be wrong). The exercise encourages the kind of deep probing required to resolve situations in which moral/legal/ ethical codes have been violated. Acknowledge that while the handout is lighthearted in nature, it is designed to encourage the kind of far-below-the-surface thinking needed by today's leaders. You may even wish to note that some believe the tragedy of 9/11 was not so much a failure of intelligence but rather a failure of the imagination.

Variation

Attributes can be listed for any number of additional programs, such as those with an emphasis on creativity, communication, sales, meeting effectiveness, and so forth.

Discussion

Do you agree with Peter Drucker's assertion that leaders know how to ask questions—the right questions? If so, what constitutes "rightness," in terms of ethical behaviors? If you disagree, state the reason for your opposition.

Quotation

"Somehow it is more difficult to be arbitrary, arrogant, or judgmental when we are looking for good questions rather than ready to give answers to whatever comes along."
—Pam Meyer

Points of Interest

Frank Navran, director of training for the Ethics Resource Center, located in Washington, D.C., cites five key motives that lead organizations to implement ethics training for *Successful Meetings* magazine: Legal, Moral, Perceptual, Pragmatic, and Change-oriented. Ask participants to analyze critically which of these motives is (or should be) motivating their own organizations.

Standing on Common Ground

DIRECTIONS

Each numbered item below talks about things leaders have in common, things they are likely to say or do in pursuit of ethical goals. The task is to scrutinize the statements. Try to figure out the common elements in the syntax of these sentences that describe leader behaviors. Dig deeply to determine which of the lettered statements following each numbered item describe the item correctly.

1. Ethical leaders don't hesitate to use books and television or movie screens to help them improve their skills, but they probably wouldn't turn to the radio for help.

   a. The first half of the sentence above alludes to visual tools; the second half does not.

   b. The first half of that sentence cites double-lettered references; the second half does not.

   c. The first half of that sentence has tools written in an alliterative manner; the second half does not.

   d. All of the above.

   e. None of the above.

2. To improve your persuasion skills as a leader, listen, report, declare, but don't compromise your values.

   a. The first half of the sentence above uses strong verbs; the second half does not.

   b. The first half of that sentence is passive; the second half is not.

   c. The first half of that sentence contains two-syllabic recommendations; the second half does not.

   d. All of the above.

   e. None of the above.

(continued)

3. As a leader, you should commit all your resources, communicate the pros and cons of your proposal, and convince using both anecdotes and statistics, but you shouldn't deviate too far from your original intention.

   a. The first half of the sentence above is parallel; the second half is not.

   b. The first half of that sentence has a series of recommendations; the second half does not.

   c. The first half of that sentence is alliterative in its recommendation; the second half is not.

   d. All of the above.

   e. None of the above.

4. As you set the parameters of your leadership project, you need to cite the alignment of resources and goals, the benefits that will accrue, and the constructs within which others will have to operate; but you don't need to generate or even explore an excessive number of possibilities.

   a. The first half of the sentence above is alpha-sequential; the second half is not.

   b. The first half of that sentence contains infinitives; the second half does not.

   c. The first half of that sentence contains a metaphor; the second half does not.

   d. All of the above.

   e. None of the above.

5. Among other things, successful leaders know how to wow their followers and to bob with buoyancy when the waves of organizational opposition threaten to overwhelm them, but they don't know how to abandon their dreams very easily.

   a. The first half of the sentence above is longer than the second half.

   b. The first half of that sentence contains a metaphor; the second half does not.

   c. The first half of that sentence contains palindromic words; the second half does not.

   d. The first half of that sentence contains alliteration; the second half does not.

   e. None of the above.

ETHICAL LEADERSHIP

False Prophets

Approximately 15 minutes

Overview

It's incumbent on all leaders, but especially those operating from an ethical base, to consider the weight their words carry. In this exercise, participants are asked to discuss the power that words have—both negative and positive. Words that are not well chosen can even become a source of ridicule for the leader.

Purpose

➤ To understand better the effects a leader's words can have.

➤ To effect realization that leaders' words cannot always be equated with truth or reality.

Group Size

Any number of individuals can participate.

Room Arrangement

No special arrangements are required.

Materials

➤ Handout 5.1, *"False Prophets"*

➤ Optional: Inexpensive pair of sunglasses

Method

1. Note that throughout history, virtually every leader who has accomplished his or her goal has encountered opposition of one sort or another. Frequently, that opposition comes from people in high positions who feel the goal is unattainable, the project not worth pursuing, and the purpose much too ambitious. These naysayers are often people with little or no vision. Ask participants for examples from history and from their own experiences that illustrate the opposition that ultimately successful leaders initially meet.

2. Distribute the handout and tell the group they can work alone or in pairs to match the naysayer with his or her nonvisionary statement. (The answers are: 1C 2I 3G 4J 5F 6A 7H 8B 9D 10E.) Award a pair of sunglasses to the person who finishes first so that he or she will not be blinded by his or her own brilliance.

3. Bring closure to the exercise by asking participants to think of history's (or their organization's) leaders and the words that have inspired others to behave in responsible, ethical ways. Consider Winston Churchill's exhortation to the British people during World War II: "Never, never, never give up." Or John F. Kennedy's assertion to potential volunteers that the Peace Corps would be the toughest job they'd ever love.

Variation

Have participants discuss the myths (listed in the Points of Interest) with which they have had personal experience.

Discussion

➤ What expert opinions have been offered about a leadership project you're currently working on?

➤ How much credence do you place in those opinions?

➤ What things *are* likely to deter you from carrying out some leadership plan?

➤ Whose words inspire you to continue?

Quotation

"The art of being wise is the art of knowing what to overlook."
—William James

Points of Interest

Leaders who inaccurately prophesize may not be unethical. It's possible they simply lack good judgment. Sometimes, too, people perpetuate myths about ethics—myths that can seriously impact the ethical decisions others are trying to make. Author Nan DeMars lists these as the most common myths about ethical behavior:

➤ "I have to do what I'm told—to keep my job!"

➤ "I can trust my boss to always be fair."

➤ "I can trust my company to always be fair."

➤ "I really made a big mistake. I'm a bad person."

➤ "What others do is none of my concern."

➤ "I'm the only one who sees what's going on—and who cares."

➤ "An action is either right or wrong."

➤ "It's not my job to police my boss."

➤ "I can't change this place."

➤ "A person cannot be talked into greater moral courage."

➤ "You are born with your morality."

➤ "Women have a more developed sense of ethics than men do."

➤ "People just naturally 'do the right thing' when presented with a moral dilemma."

➤ "Good employees don't do bad things. People act unethically because they are selfish, stupid, or bad."

➤ "Ethical management means ethical organizations."

Reprinted with permission from *You Want Me To Do What? When/Where & How to Draw the Line at Work* (Simon & Schuster) by Nan DeMars, Office Ethics Trainer/Consultant, President of Executary Services, a seminar/search/office ethics consultant firm in Minneapolis.

False Prophets

DIRECTIONS

It's hard, but certainly not impossible, to remain stalwart in the face of opposition, especially when that face is speaking with the voice of authority. Authorities, though, are not always right in their opinion and not always right in their motivation for offering that opinion. Take a look at these opinions. Make a prediction about the well-known authority or expert who may have made each statement. Then, see if your list of predicted experts matches the actual experts at the bottom of the page. Even if you didn't guess all the actual experts, proceed next to match the bottom-page experts to the following ten statements.

___ 1. "The atomic bomb will not go off. And I speak as an expert in explosives."

___ 2. "What can be more palpably absurd than the prospect held out of locomotives traveling twice as fast as stagecoaches?"

___ 3. "Babe Ruth made a big mistake when he gave up pitching."

___ 4. "The telephone is an amazing invention, but who would ever want to use one of them?"

___ 5. "People will soon get tired of staring at a plywood box every night."

___ 6. "There is no reason for any individual to have a computer in their home."

___ 7. "I was told that I wasn't big enough, maybe not fast enough and not strong enough."

___ 8. *"Gone with the Wind* is going to be the biggest flop in the history of Hollywood. I'm just glad it'll be Clark Gable who's falling flat on his face and not me."

___ 9. "Who the hell wants to hear actors talk?"

___ 10. "While a calculator is now equipped with 18,000 vacuum tubes and weighs 30 tons, computers in the future may have only 1,000 vacuum tubes and only weigh one and a half tons."

A. Ken Olson, former president of Digital Equipment Corporation   B. Gary Cooper   C. Admiral W. Leahy   D. Harry Warner, founder of Warner Brothers Studios, in 1927   E. 1949 issue of *Popular Mechanics*   F. Darryl F. Zanuck, former head of 20th Century Fox   G. Tris Speaker, Hall of Fame outfielder   H. Wayne Gretzky   I. *The Quarterly Review*, England, in March 1825   J. President Rutherford B. Hayes

Park Your Ethicar in the Harvard Yard

6

Approximately 45 minutes

Overview

A quarter of a century ago, Harvard undertook a study of why businesspeople behave unethically. In this exercise, participants list reasons for unethical behavior. They are then asked to prioritize their reasons as a small group and to compare their answers to those provided decades ago.

Purpose

To provoke thought and discussion regarding root causes of unethical behavior.

Group Size

Any number of individuals can participate. Participants will first work alone and then in small groups.

Room Arrangement

If possible, table groups for four or five participants.

Materials

➤ Projector for transparencies or PowerPoint slides

➤ Transparency 6.1, *"Six Reasons Businesspeople Act Unethically"*

➤ Optional: Newspaper articles related to business ethics

Method

1. Begin with a brief discussion of current events related to business ethics. If possible, distribute the newspaper articles and allow a few moments for cursory review.

2. Next, ask participants, working alone, to list six possible reasons for unethical behavior among business people.

3. Divide the audience into groups of four or five and ask them to share their answers and then to select the six most likely reasons. As a group, they will prioritize these reasons.

4. When they've finished, show the transparency and ask the small groups to compare their answers to a recent report from *ABC News*.

5. Lead a discussion of the similarities and differences participants noted. There will probably be considerable overlap, as greed, for example is what is driving today's most notable corporate transgressors. However, some interesting ideas may emerge from participants—ideas that are not the obvious reasons. Someone might list, for example, the influence of movies that make heroes/anti-heroes out of unethical businesspeople (Michael Douglas told us that "Greed is good" in *Wall Street*).

6. Ask each group to prepare a realistic plan of action that a leader could use to get at the root cause of unethical behavior and to eliminate it.

Variation

Ask participants to devise a survey for use in their own organization. The survey should not only elicit reasons but should also ask respondents to select possible ways of creating a more ethical culture.

Discussion

➤ How much has really changed in terms of the reasons for unethical practices?

➤ What forces could lead to a change for the better?

➤ To what extent can a leader influence others to change?

Quotation

"Time is a dressmaker specializing in alterations."
—Faith Baldwin

Points of Interest

No one will ever argue that businesses are not in business to make money. Yet moneymaking is not the only value for ethics-driven organizations. Consider Legg Mason, a holding company headquartered in Baltimore. They engage in securities brokerage, trading, investment management, and underwriting.

Chip Mason, former chair, regarded honesty as the Number 1 principle on which his company operated. Second was an insistence that customers make a lot of money, and third, that brokers should not be greedy. In the words of authors Michael Mescon and Timothy Mescon, "Mason's personal code has become the professional code for the entire organization. . . ."

Discuss with participants/leaders what their personal code is and how far it extends into their organizations.

SIX REASONS BUSINESSPEOPLE ACT UNETHICALLY

1. Rationalization
2. Bad role models in the organization
3. Peer pressure
4. Difficulty in defining what is ethical
5. Corporate culture
6. Pressure from superiors

from "What Is Ethical: Politics, Circumstances, Excuses Can Blur What is Right" by Michael S. Jones, ABCNews.com, February 21, 2002

ETHICAL LEADERSHIP

You Don't Need Leaders to Tell People the Good News

7

Approximately 45 minutes (more, if the group is large)

Overview

You need leaders, according to Lee Iacocca, to tell people things they don't want to hear and then get them to do things they don't want to do. The "right thing" is not always the easy thing. As Rudy Giuliani told us, we had to live in defiance of our fear following the destruction of the World Trade Center by terrorists. The right thing may also involve sacrifice: President Kennedy asked Americans to temporarily give up comfort in order to serve the less fortunate in foreign countries.

This exercise requires participants, working alone, to complete a comparison matrix. It then challenges them to think of a difficult-to-swallow message derived from the matrix and to strategize how that message can be made digestible.

Purpose

➤ To elicit thoughts regarding best ethical practices.

➤ To develop awareness of the gap between the ideal and the real in work-related scenarios.

➤ To outline a message that might close the ethical gap.

Group Size

Any number of participants can engage in this exercise. Participants first work alone and then make a short presentation to three others.

**Room
Arrangement**

Flexible seating, if possible, so that participants can form small groups after working alone on the first part of the exercise.

Materials

Handout 7.1, *"Comparison Matrix"*

Procedure

1. Remind the group of management guru Tom Peters's advice: "If you have gone a whole week without being disobedient, you are not serving yourself or your company well." Discuss the possible meanings of "disobedient."

2. Note that one possible meaning is to express dissatisfaction with the organizational status quo, in an effort to promote continuous improvement.

3. Distribute the handout and ask participants to fill it out. (*Note:* If you spot some people struggling with the best practices for the first column, quietly suggest they work with another person. Avoid possible embarrassment with a comment such as, "That's the part I had the most trouble with myself. I had to call a colleague for help. Do you mind if I have you and _____ work together on this?")

4. Once the handout is complete, ask participants, still working alone, to outline a brief "speech" they would make to their manager or other high-level organizational leader to explain the need to remove a specific barrier and would suggest ways the removal could be implemented. The speech should last 5 minutes, at the very most.

5. Next, have participants form groups of four. Each person in the subgroup will deliver his or her speech and will receive feedback from the others in the group.

6. Bring closure to the exercise by asking what it would take for these speeches to actually be delivered.

Variation

This exercise could easily be adapted for:

➤ Presentation programs (for which participants would actually deliver the speech).

➤ Leadership programs (for which participants would develop a proposal and work to have it approved and then implemented).

➤ Communications programs (for which participants would employ specific persuasion tools, such as those described in the Points of Interest).

Discussion _____

➤ In what ways have you "defied" the status quo in recent months in order to achieve an improved or more ethical state of affairs?

➤ One definition of a "leader" is the person who takes others where they would not have gone without him or her. To what places do people in your organization need to "travel" along the ethical road?

➤ How else could you use a gap analysis to effect improvement in your organization as far as ethical practices as concerned?

Quotation _____

"All that really matters is devotion to something bigger than ourselves."
—Teilhard de Chardin

Points of Interest _____

Keep in mind these D-words as you work to persuade others to adapt your recommendations:

➤ **Drama**—Heighten the emotional appeal of your presentation by adding a bit of drama to it. The excitement could appear in your voice, in your body language, or in the content of your remarks. A surprising statistic is just one of the ways you could add depth and texture to your message.

➤ **Developments**—Relating current events (both inside and outside the organization) to the need for the change you are proposing is an effective means of persuasion. You can use the events to validate the likelihood of success of your idea or to suggest a given outcome could be avoided if your plan were implemented.

➤ **Deprecation (self only)**—At the 2002 Academy Awards presentation, Woody Allen told the audience that he offered the names of 14 other filmmakers who would be even better representatives of New York City than he himself. Then he told them that a caller admitted they had already tried the others and none of them were available. Such humor almost always serves to develop a rapport with an audience. Translated into a business setting, participants might say something like this prior to making their proposal to their manager: *"I envy the experience you have in this industry. Even though I'm relatively new, I think I've come up with a way we could improve the communication flow in our office."*

Comparison Matrix

DIRECTIONS

Begin by listing, as specifically as possible, five of the best practices in which leaders should engage, in your opinion. In the second column, do a reality check: indicate the extent to which one or more leaders in your organization are executing each of these practices. Finally, specify the barriers that would have to be removed or the steps that would have to be taken if the gap between the ideal and the real were to be closed.

For example, a top executive had to forget $1.1 million of his 2002 bonus for including false information on his resume ("Zarella forfeits a million at B&L," *Democrat & Chronicle,* October 30, 2002, page 1a). If best practices include having truthful official biographies and if your company currently does not verify the accuracy of such information, the HR department would have to conduct further research on candidates for top positions.

Best Leadership Practices	Current Practices	Barriers/Steps
1.		
2.		
3.		
4.		
5.		

8 Machiavellian, Manipulative, or Masterful?

Approximately 30 minutes

Overview

This exercise begins with a quiz that, ideally, helps participants realize that Machiavellian, and even manipulative, behavior can actually benefit all parties involved. They then work in pairs to discuss what they would have done in two real-world situations.

Purpose

➤ To relate Machiavellian principles to positive business practices.

➤ To stimulate discussion of ethically appropriate behavior.

Group Size

Any number of participants can engage in this exercise, which calls initially for individual work and then paired discussions.

Room Arrangement

No special arrangements are required.

Materials

➤ Handout 8.1, *"Historical Applications"*

➤ Handout 8.2, *"How Machiavellian Are You?"*

➤ Handout 8.3, *"What Would You Do?"*

Procedure

1. Conduct a short discussion regarding the importance of open-mindedness in those who would lead. (You may choose to cite the example of Roger Boisjolie, a junior engineer, who tried repeatedly, but unsuccessfully, to warn his superiors of a problem with the O-ring in the Challenger shuttle.)

2. Explain that the handout you are distributing (Handout 8.1, "Historical Applications") will afford them an opportunity to learn if they can look beyond certain negative connotations in order to find the value in a given set of circumstances.

3. After they complete the test, distribute Handout 8.2 ("How Machiavellian Are You?") and allow a few minutes for participants to read the interpretation of the exercise results. Discuss the fact that we often recoil from certain words (or people or situations) without fully exploring the possible value inherent in those contexts.

4. Next, distribute Handout 8.3 ("What Would You Do?") and ask participants to work in pairs to complete it.

5. Debrief with an exchange that acknowledges the following points:

   a. It may be absolutely ethical for a leader to engage in behavior that is "Machiavellian" (in the broadest sense of the word) and even in behavior that is manipulative.

   b. We need to examine words as carefully as we examine situations. People who are comfortable with power, for example, need not be "power-hungry." In fact, the work of Harvard professor David McClelland shows that our best leaders, in fact, have a strong need for power.

   c. It's important for leaders to explore both the connotative and denotative meanings lying below the surface of words, people, and circumstances.

   d. Moral dilemmas are dilemmas precisely because there's seldom a black-or-white answer. While we must acknowledge that people have the right to do what they believe is the "right thing to do," we must also acknowledge that in-depth discussions may help those people refine the choices they are about to make.

Variation

Icebreaker: Divide participants into small groups and ask them to share labels they have been identified with over the years (for example, "worrywart"). Then have each person explain the potential merit in that word—citing, perhaps, a time when they were very grateful that they *did* worry over the details someone else might have ignored. Move from the concept of positive-aspects-of-negative-designations to the exercise on Machiavellian behavior. Note that such behavior is not necessarily a bad thing to engage in. In fact, with a lofty ideal guiding it, such behavior could be regarded as thoroughly ethical.

Discussion

➤ What other words (other than "Machiavellian," "manipulative," and "power-hungry") are generally viewed as having a negative connotation?

➤ What merit could lie behind some of these words?

➤ How open are the lines of communication and consideration in your own organization? Are leaders unethically hoarding knowledge in the hopes of making themselves more powerful? Are they withholding information in order to deceive? Are they digging into what words really mean, even when it may be time-consuming or painful to do so? (To illustrate, quality guru Philip Crosby maintains that you can ask 10 different people what the word "quality" means and receive 10 different answers.) It is wrong for leaders to assume they alone have a corner on the word-meaning market.

Quotation

"We are all of us all the time coming together and falling apart. The point is we are not rocks. Who wants to be one anyway, impermeable, unchanging, our history already played out. . . ."
—John Rosenthal

Points of Interest

An article by marketing consultant and speaker Terry Mandel encourages us to revisit the meaning of the word *competition.* He suggests that by moving from an us-versus-them mindset and toward the original meaning of the word—"striving together"—we can regard competitors as mirrors reflecting a direction in which we should be moving.

Historical Applications

DIRECTIONS

Read the following statements and answer **Agree** or **Disagree,** depending on the extent to which you agree with the truth of the statement. Think of the degree to which the statement matches your way of thinking. If you both agree and disagree with a given statement, try to determine which choice you'd agree with just slightly more than the other choice. Instead of a 50/50 response, then, you would consider the statement as a choice between 51/49 percent; you would favor one response slightly more than the other. (There are no trick questions here. Simply tell if you agree or disagree with the statements.)

Place a check ☑ in the appropriate box to the right of each statement.

	Agree	Disagree
1. We should be adaptable when unforeseen events occur.	❏	❏
2. One change always leaves indentations on which to build another change.	❏	❏
3. In the beginning, problems are easy to cure but hard to diagnose; with the passage of time, having gone unrecognized and unattended, they become easy to diagnose, but hard to cure.	❏	❏
4. A workplace accustomed to freedom is more easily managed by its own employees than by any other arrangement.	❏	❏
5. A wise influencer must always tread the path of great men and women and should imitate those who have excelled.	❏	❏
6. People who least rely on luck alone will be the most successful.	❏	❏
7. Success is a combination of opportunity and ability.	❏	❏

(continued)

	Agree	Disagree
8. Most people have no faith in new things until they have been proven by experiences.	❑	❑
9. If you have to beg others to fulfill a mission, you are destined to fail.	❑	❑
10. If you are respected, you will be secure, honored, and successful.	❑	❑
11. Things that come easily are hard to maintain. Things that are hard won are easier to maintain.	❑	❑
12. A leader who thinks more about his or her own interests than about yours, who seeks his or her own advantage for everything he or she does, will never be a good leader, for others will never be able to trust him or her.	❑	❑
13. To keep employees loyal, managers must honor them by sharing both distinctions and duties.	❑	❑

How Machiavellian Are You?

INTERPRETATION

Because there are 13 items, if you had 7 or more in one category, then that is your "majority" category. Which category, **Agree** or **Disagree,** is your majority category? _____

Now let's see how open you are to influences that do not represent typical sources of knowledge acquisition. In all likelihood, you agreed with at least 7 of the statements. Would it "shock" you to learn that these 13 paraphrased statements are taken from *The Prince* by Niccolo Machiavelli? Written 500 years ago, the book has become synonymous with words such as "duplicity" and "deceit." Yet, much of what it endorses makes sense for today's leader, manager, and/or influencer.

Does a majority of **Agree** answers mean you are Machiavellian, in the most negative sense of the word? No, not at all. It means simply that no one thing is 100 percent "right" or 100 percent "wrong." Even in *The Prince* there is wisdom from which we can profit. But . . . if you are not open, you won't be able to spot the worth; your stamp of "worthless" will prevent you from seeing worth in hard realities. If you take no risks into the unpopular or unknown, you will not be able to optimize or reify possibilities that lie hidden in the here and now.

Remember that selling a particular service, product, or proposal to others depends on your understanding of the current reality and your ability to remain mentally flexible or open to new ideas. Not until you have achieved these mental states can you create the new reality. It's often true that "if you build it, they will come," but if you don't hear or see the opportunities calling to you, you will never be able to turn them into new realities.

What Would You Do?

DIRECTIONS

"Doing the right thing" involves making tough choices. What's "right" for one person may be wrong for another—even though the given action might be totally within the bounds of propriety and policy. In the blank space beneath each scenario, tell what course of action you would have taken and why. Be prepared to answer the questions that follow each real-life case study, too. Determine if the person in the case study used masterful behavior. Consider whether or not the behavior reflected the positive or negative aspects of Machiavellianism and/or manipulation.

1. Brenda believed she had to work harder than most men to make it in her company, a major defense contractor. She worked hard, perhaps harder than she had to, and let her work speak for itself. She was often described as a straight-shooting, no-nonsense manager whose loyalty to the firm and whose honesty were impeccable. She made progress but didn't reach the levels she had set as goals for herself by a certain time. She was discussing the situation one day with Judy, another manager who was moving very rapidly along her own career path. In an effort to be helpful, Judy suggested if Brenda were willing to use her "feminine wiles," she could move ahead more rapidly.

   If you were Brenda, what would you have done? _____

   _____

   _____

   _____

   a. Are there ethical issues involved in using one's feminine or masculine "wiles"? If so, what are they?

b. What are the criteria by which people move rapidly ahead in a corporate setting?

c. Relate this statement by Don Petersen, former head of Ford Motor Company—*"Results depend on relationships"*—to this situation.

2. Mark was known throughout the department as being a "stand-up kind of guy"—respected by everyone for his honesty, trustworthiness, and dependability. Jerry Fletcher, his boss, asked to see him one day and explained that he had heard "rumblings" about the sexist behavior of a particular employee—behavior that was not visible whenever Jerry was in the vicinity. Despite Jerry's frequently stated policy about sexual harassment, Jerry suspected the lack of formal complaint didn't mean there was no problem. He worried that one day, someone would simply decide enough was enough and would file a lawsuit. Consequently, he asked Mark to spy on the employee and to report back to him.

If you were Mark, what would you have done? _____

_____

_____

_____

a. What possible reasons could explain why there might be no formal complaints in a situation like this?

b. What does the law state regarding behaviors that constitute sexual harassment?

c. On what factors should Mark base his decision to do or not do what his boss is asking?

9

Be-Guile

Approximately 25 minutes

Overview

Participants are asked to think like leaders in this exercise and to consider changes they believe are needed in their organizations to improve the ethical climate. They provide three ideas in each of three categories and then draft a letter to their manager proposing the one change they believe is most critical.

Purpose

➤ To encourage thinking about necessary organizational changes related to ethics.

➤ To encourage action that might result in the change actually taking place.

Group Size

Any number of participants can engage in this exercise. Participants will first work alone and then with two others. (Note: The exercise works best if participants are all from the same organization.)

Room Arrangement

Any classroom setup will work for this exercise.

Materials

➤ Handout 9.1, *"Let It Be"*

➤ Circular adhesive dots

➤ **Optional:** Token prizes, such as pens, for members of the winning triad

Procedure

Open by asking for a show of hands in response to these questions:

1. How many of you enjoy change? How many of you think the average employee fears change? How many of you create change?

2. Ask a participant who raised his or her hand for all three questions to come forward and serve as a discussion leader. Participants will raise questions regarding change, for example, "Why do you enjoy change?" "Why do you think so many other people fear it?" "What change have you recently instituted?" "How can we encourage others to accept change?" "What, in your opinion and experience, is the relationship between change and risk?"

3. Once the discussion leader has responded from a personal perspective, thank him or her, and step in as the new discussion leader. Start the discussion with questions such as: "What are some changes you feel are necessary in your department as far as ethics or values are concerned?" "In your organization?" "Why are these changes not taking place?"

4. Once you feel participants are thinking along the lines of needed ethical change, distribute the handout and allow 5 to 10 minutes for its completion.

5. Ask participants to review what they've written and to select the one change-item they feel should be implemented the most.

6. Have participants work with two others. Have the triad discuss their choices and then have them vote on the one change-item (among the three) that the triad feels is most critical.

7. Have the triads work together to compose a letter that, ideally, would convince a member of senior management to institute the necessary change. Ask them to write as legibly as possible and not to put their names (or their managers' names) on the letters.

8. Post the letters around the room.

9. Distribute one adhesive dot to each participant with the instruction to vote for the letter they feel would most convince management to take action. (They will vote by affixing their dot to the letter of their choice.)

10. Award prizes or at least applaud the triad with the winning letter. Read it aloud, perhaps more than once, and debrief by asking participants what specific elements they found compelling.

11. Conclude with a reference to Ken Blanchard's quotation (below).

Variation

Invite a member of senior management to read the posted letters, instead of having participants do so. Have the manager decide which is the one he or she would be most likely to take action on. Ask for input regarding the content/context that encouraged that action.

Discussion

➤ What prevents people from taking action on things that clearly need to be improved?

➤ Under what conditions are you most inspired or motivated to get things done?

➤ Does guilt ever play a role in encouraging action?

Quotation

"The key to leadership today is influence, not authority."
—Ken Blanchard

Points of Inerest

In some ways, the environment is much like the weather: everyone talks about it but not everyone does something about it. Not so for SET Laboratories, Inc., of Mulino, Oregon. When the company ships software, they depend on real popcorn instead of fake peanuts—the polystyrene kind. Not only is the popcorn better for the environment, it even costs less—by 60 percent.

Let It Be

DIRECTIONS

Think about your own team, work unit, department, or even your own organization or industry. Think especially about ethical issues or problems that need resolution or solution.

➤ What are some changes that ought to be made? List three of these changes in the first column below.

➤ Next, consider some changes that "have got" to be implemented, even though you may not have a part in that implementation, and/or you don't know when that implementation might occur. Think in terms of critically important changes that warrant immediate attention. List three of these changes in the second column.

➤ Finally, regard changes that you can put in place yourself. List three of these changes that would be within your power to institute. These should be changes that you feel strongly about—so strongly that you can actually make a commitment to implementing them. In the third column, list three things that are going to be different from now on.

Oughtta Be	Gotta Be	Gonna Be

ETHICAL LEADERSHIP

10 More P-O-W-E-R to You

Approximately 45 minutes

Overview

Words beginning with each of the letters that spell *power* are listed for discussion purposes. Participants first make individual choices and then attempt to reach group consensus. The same process is then used as participants react to statements about ethical leadership.

PURPOSE

➤ To spark ideas about the ethical correlations between power and leadership.

➤ To challenge participants to reach consensus about leadership statements.

Group Size

Any number of participants can engage in this exercise, which has two parts. In each part, participants first work alone and then as part of a group.

Room Arrangement

Flexible seating, if possible, so that participants can form subgroups twice during the exercise.

Materials

➤ Flipchart and marking pens
➤ Handout 10.1, *"Leading a Group"*

Procedure

1. Write the letters P–O–W–E–R on the flipchart.

2. Ask participants, working alone, to come up with three words, beginning with the letter "p," that relate to either leadership and/or ethics. Next, they will think of three words starting with the letter "o" that also relate to leadership and/or to

ethics. They will continue in this manner with the letters "w,"
"e," and "r."

3. After approximately 10 minutes, ask participants to determine
   which of all those words is the most important for a person
   practicing ethical leadership. They should place a checkmark
   in front of that word on their papers.

4. Ask the class to form groups of four or five. Each person will
   advocate for his or her word, trying to persuade the others
   that this one word is the most critical element of ethical
   leadership. The group will attempt to reach consensus on the
   one word that is most relevant or critical to the practice of
   ethical leadership. At the very least, group members will have
   an opportunity to explore aspects of ethical leadership. At
   best, such exploration will simultaneously serve as an exercise
   in consensus-building.

5. Call on each team to tell the selected word and write the
   various words on the flipchart, commenting on each as you do
   so.

6. Distribute the handout and ask participants to write their
   Agree or Disagree answers on the left-hand column only.

7. Next, form different groups of four or five this time, with
   participants moving to different seats. Ask the groups to work
   on completing the right-hand column of the handout. Groups
   should work towards consensus on the statements regarding
   leadership.

8. Debrief by asking a spokesperson from each group to describe
   briefly the process employed. After each person finishes, ask
   pertinent questions about the way power was used (if it was at
   all) as the groups worked to reach full agreement. Allude to
   the ethical use of power and the importance of having leaders
   who do not dominate or overpower others. Draw parallels
   among and between such words as "harmony," "cooperation,"
   "participative leadership," "equal voices," and so on.

Variation

Appoint an observer for each group as they work to achieve
consensus. Have the observers look specifically for participants
who demonstrate leadership by suggesting compromise positions
that might enable the group to reach accord about the
statements. For example, the observer would be looking for
someone who suggests altering the wording. (The directions do

not prohibit such action.) Afterwards, ask the observers to meet for a few moments outside the room and to appoint one spokesperson who will make general comments about a leader's ability to achieve agreement, as reflected in this microcosmic assignment.

Discussion

➤ Beyond the obvious abuse-of-power answer, why does the word "power" carry such negative connotations?

➤ To what extent do you feel leaders should enjoy exercising power?

➤ How would you define "power"?

Quotation

"Tell the truth, but make the truth fascinating."
—David Ogilvy

Points of Interest

As reported in *The Economist,* Harvard began offering courses in business ethics back in 1915. Today, it is rare for business programs not to include such courses. One business school sends MBA students to a monastery for a few weeks of soul-searching. Consider ways organizations can encourage such searches without having employees leave the premises.

Leading a Group

DIRECTIONS

First read each statement and tell if you agree or disagree with it. Circle the letter "A" or "D" in the left-hand column to indicate how you feel about each statement. Then, work with four or five others, attempt to reach consensus on each of the statements, and circle the corresponding letter in the right-hand column.

Individual			Group	
A	D	1. The purpose of leadership is to develop other leaders.	A	D
A	D	2. As an employee of my organization, I feel my leadership opportunities are limited.	A	D
A	D	3. It's hard to exercise leadership over others because most employees are simply interested in earning their salary, not in contributing to the organization.	A	D
A	D	4. It's hard to exert leadership because the people above us don't listen to us.	A	D
A	D	5. People who use power well tend to have big egos.	A	D
A	D	6. To be an effective leader, you must have some drive toward self-aggrandizement.	A	D
A	D	7. People who strive to be leaders are primarily interested in advancing their own careers.	A	D
A	D	8. Leaders are born, not made.	A	D
A	D	9. "Change agent" is a phrase that could be substituted for "leader."	A	D
A	D	10. A good leader must be a good communicator.	A	D

Ethical Workplace Conduct

INTRODUCTION
Ethical Workplace Conduct

THOMAS J. MITRANO

When I was in law school, we used to have heated debates about whether corporations should—or even could—be held to the same standards as human citizens are. Today, thinking back to those days, I'm reminded of the intense and risky fight Ansel Adams, Imogen Cunningham, Edward Weston, and others waged over whether photography could be considered an art form.

Today, such debates seem almost quaint. Of course photography is an art form. Of course corporations are subject to standards of fairness and legality just as flesh-and-blood citizens are.

Still, for many years, the "citizenship" of corporations was significant mostly for tax, accounting, and business operations matters. Although these concerns continue, the growing focus on the day-to-day implications of citizenship for entities created by law, not DNA, raises complex issues, both profound and everyday, for all of us who manage, enter into relationships with, or are otherwise affected by our fellow corporate citizens.

In many respects, legislation and the courts provide answers to many basic questions raised by the existence of rights and privileges of corporations. For years, the common law has denied wrongdoing corporate directors, shareholders, and owner-managers the synthetic protection of the "corporate veil." The venerable Employee Retirement Income Security Act (ERISA) and its regulations impose extensive sets of rules aimed at imposing a fairness standard when companies create retirement programs for their staff. Employment and hiring practices legislation, civil rights laws, gender equity, and sexual-preferences cases are all aimed at bringing a legal abstraction, the "corporation," down to earth by defining the duties and social mores with which corporations must comply in relationships with individuals.

The Foreign Corrupt Practices Act has tackled the ethically and culturally complex area of standards for business practices for our corporate citizens all over the world. Criminal actions against vast international corporations and their auditors and attorneys seek to overlay a very real set of criminal consequences onto the decision-making and operations of even the largest organizations.

But the exploration of the meaning of citizenship for corporations does not stop with the legal, judicial, legislative, regulatory, or criminal infrastructure of our society. In fact, for most of us, day-to-day, there are many more practical issues that concern us. How does a good corporate citizen "write and circulate e-mail"? Can a corporate employer eavesdrop on staff members' communications with impunity? Should corporate citizens be under a greater duty to balance business with humanity's environmental needs than noncorporate citizens? What exactly are the burdens of being bigger than any other kid on the block (by virtue of being able to concentrate vast resources)?

Human scale issues such as privacy, patriotism, initiative, reputation, candor, ego, anger, and loss are being examined anew today as we consider implications at the corporate citizen level.

The well equipped employee, manager, and person in the street today need a new competence and literacy in, as well as a new attitude toward, issues such as these.

The following chapter's objective is to develop that competence and introduce that literacy. By thoughtfully considering the issues and working through the exercises, the involved reader will assume a competence-based, proactive position able to deal with, manage, and mutually benefit from relationships with fellow corporate citizens.

THOMAS J. MITRANO, ESQ., is General Counsel and Principal at AM Partners, Inc., an internationally recognized architecture, interiors, planning, and graphics firm located in Honolulu, Hawaii. A resident of Hawaii since 1982, Mr. Mitrano is a graduate of the University of Toronto (1968) and Harvard Law School (1972). He is admitted to practice law in Hawaii, California, and before several federal courts. Mr. Mitrano has practiced at law offices in New York, Tokyo, Los Angeles, and Carmel, California. He has taught corporate, business, and commercial law courses.

Mr. Mitrano is also a consultant and business professional with development, managerial, operational, and planning expertise applied in the high-tech, architecture, and visitor industries; in banking; and in the nonprofit sector. He is an accomplished writer, speaker, and legislative lobbyist, with a high-level, non-native speaker's competency in reading, writing, and speaking Mandarin Chinese.

ETHICAL WORKPLACE CONDUCT

Verbally Abusive Behavior

Eve Strella and Gwen Martone

Approximately 60 to 90 minutes

Overview

Participants are encouraged to think about the ethical ramifications of verbally abusive behavior or situations in the work environment.

Purpose

To make participants aware of how verbally abusive behaviors affect job performance, organizational perspectives, and interpersonal relationships.

Group Size

The ideal group size is 18 to 20 participants.

Room Arrangement

Select a room large enough for a subgroup to break out. Set up the main work area in a "U" shape, allowing room for the facilitator to enter the "U" and be in the middle of the discussions.

Materials

➤ Projector for transparencies or for PowerPoint slides
➤ Transparencies 11.1 through 11.7 showing questions
➤ Tape for hanging the flipchart sheets on the wall
➤ Magic markers
➤ Post-it® notes (3 × 3-inch size), in bright colors if possible. You will need one pad of notes for each table.

➤ Flipchart with the activity headings written at the top of each page. (As the pages are completed, they should be hung on the wall for viewing.) Use a Post-it® note or piece of paper to conceal the heading "Your Home Life" on the third flipchart page.

Headings and setup for flipchart sheets:

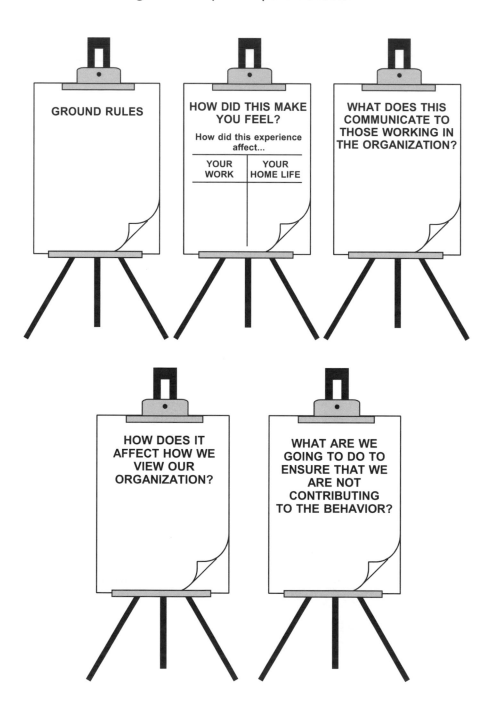

GROUND RULES

HOW DID THIS MAKE YOU FEEL?

How did this experience affect...

YOUR WORK	YOUR HOME LIFE

WHAT DOES THIS COMMUNICATE TO THOSE WORKING IN THE ORGANIZATION?

HOW DOES IT AFFECT HOW WE VIEW OUR ORGANIZATION?

WHAT ARE WE GOING TO DO TO ENSURE THAT WE ARE NOT CONTRIBUTING TO THE BEHAVIOR?

Procedure

1. Spend the first 5 minutes establishing ground rules with participants. These rules encourage a more open environment, permitting individuals to share their thoughts without feeling they are overstepping bounds. The rules might deal with confidentiality, for example: *"What is shared in the room stays in the room"* and *"No names—company or people."* After you go over the ground rules, tape this sheet on the wall. The second flipchart page is not visible at this time.

2. Show and read the question on transparency 1, *"How many of you have witnessed verbally abusive situations in your workplace?"* Ask participants to pair up to share their experiences with one another for 5 to 10 minutes.

3. Next, facilitate a discussion for approximately 10 minutes by inviting the group as a whole to share experiences. Show and read the question on the second transparency, *"How many of you have personally experienced verbal abuse?"* to stimulate the discussion. **Note:** Be prepared for emotions to surface during this part of the exercise. Intercede if you observe any participant becoming emotional; say something like: *"Before you finish, let me share with you an experience of my own"* to allow the participant to compose him- or herself. Of course, you could also ask, *"Would you prefer to tell us the rest of this terrible story later?"*

4. Proceed to the next question on transparency 3, *"How did this make you feel?"* Refer to the flipchart sheet with the same heading at the top. This part of the exercise calls for participants to answer the question individually and silently. Instruct them to write their feelings on the Post-it® notes (one comment per sheet). Invite participants to share what they've written and then to hang the Post-it® notes on the flipchart sheet. Facilitate any discussion that takes place at this time. When the discussion is complete, take the flipchart sheet and tape it to the wall.

5. Show the next transparency, 4, and ask the question, *"How did this affect your work?"* The flipchart page will be set up as a "T" chart with "Your Home Life" covered up at this time. In this part of the exercise participants work alone. Instruct them to write their comments on the Post-it® notes (one per sheet). After a few minutes, invite the participants to share what they've written and then to hang the Post-it® notes on the flipchart sheet. Facilitate any discussion that takes place at this time.

6. Show transparency 5 and ask the question, *"How did this affect your home life?"* Uncover the right side of the "T" chart on the flipchart titled "Your Home Life." This portion of the exercise, once again, is completed individually. Instruct the participants to write their comments on the Post-it® notes (one per sheet). Encourage discussion among participants of what they've written and then invite them to hang the Post-it® notes on the flipchart sheet. When this discussion is complete, tape the flipchart page to the wall.

7. Place transparency 6 on the overhead and ask the question, *"When this behavior is allowed to continue, what does this communicate to those working in the organization?"* Ask participants to pair up and share with one another what they feel is communicated and why. Instruct them next to write their comments on the Post-it® notes (one per sheet). Facilitate any discussion that arises at this time. Ask participants to place their Post-it® notes on the flipchart page. When the discussion is complete, tape the flipchart page to the wall.

8. Continue with the question on transparency 7, *"When this behavior is allowed to continue, how does it affect how we view our organization?"* Ask participants to form pairs and share with one another specifically how such behavior and the fact that it's allowed to occur affect their view of the organization. Instruct them to write their comments on the Post-it® notes (one per sheet). Invite participants to share their thoughts and then to hang the Post-it® notes on the flipchart sheet. Facilitate any discussion that takes place at this time. When the discussion winds down, place this flipchart sheet onto the wall.

9. Conclude by asking the participants, *"What have you learned through this exercise?"* Facilitate the discussion and bring in key points of interest from the flipchart sheets hanging on the wall. Then ask the question, on the final flipchart page, *"With what we have learned today about how abusive behaviors affect us at work and at home, what are we going to do to ensure that we are not contributing to this behavior?"* Facilitate an open discussion and write comments on a flipchart sheet.

Discussion

➤ Does your organization have a policy regarding violence in the workplace? If so, what does it say about verbally abusive behavior?

➤ If not, what should it say about such behavior?

Quotations

"Be the change you want to see in others."
—Mahatma Gandhi

"Everything I do and say with anyone makes a difference."
—Gita Bellin

"Everyone and everything around you is your teacher."
—Ken Keyes, Jr.

Points of Interest

It doesn't take much imagination to realize that verbally abusive behavior can easily move from a verbal altercation to physical blows. The statistics concerning violence in the workplace are truly alarming.

The Federal Bureau of Labor Statistics Report from August 2001 notes the total fatalities within the workplace is 5,915. Homicides attributable to shooting account for 9 percent of that number and all other causes of homicide total an additional 2 percent. (See www.bls.gov.)

Furthermore, the National Safe Workplace Institute (NSWPI) reports that nearly 25 percent of all employees report having been threatened, harassed, or actually attacked on the job in recent years.

Two million employees report physical attacks. The cost of these attacks, in lost work and legal expenses alone, is nearing $40 billion. The actual cost may be higher: 55 percent of victims indicate they failed to report incidents to the police department.

ILLUMINATE OF ROCHESTER, INC., is a coaching, consulting, training, and team development organization whose focus is to assist individuals and organizations in transition through issues of change, layoffs, mergers, abusive management and co-worker behavior, and fear in the workplace. Co-CEOs Eve Strella and Gwen Martone have merged their expertise as an industrial engineer and a clinical therapist with a combined 32 years of hands-on experience in the area of human solutions.

How many of you have witnessed verbally abusive situations in your workplace?

How many of you
have personally
experienced verbal
abuse?

How did this make you feel?

How did this affect your work?

How did this affect your home life?

When this behavior is allowed to continue, what does this communicate to those working in the organization?

When this behavior is allowed to continue, how does it affect how we view our organization?

ETHICAL WORKPLACE CONDUCT

E-Mail Ethics

12

Approximately 15 minutes

Overview

Participants are encouraged to think about the ethical consequences of seemingly innocent acts, such as circulating humorous Internet lists to co-workers.

Purpose

To make participants aware of negative consequences associated with misuse of the Internet.

Group Size

Any number of individuals can participate. The group should be divided into subgroups of three or four.

Room Arrangement

If possible, arrange table groups for four participants each.

Materials

➤ Transparency 12.1, *"Internet and Productivity"*

➤ Projector for transparencies or for PowerPoint slides

➤ Handout 12.1, *"What's Your EQ (Electronic Quotient)?"*

➤ Copies, if possible, of the organization's e-mail policy

Procedure

1. Begin by asking if anyone has recently received any good lists at work. These would be funny composites of responses to questions such as, "How Can You Tell You're Getting Old?" or "Ways to Get Back at the Boss" or "25 Things You Should Never Tell Your Spouse." Allow a minute or two for sharing.

2. Then show the questions on Transparency 12.1, *"Internet and Productivity."* Ask participants to pair up and discuss one or two of the questions for about 5 minutes. (Note: If copies of

the organization's Internet/e-mail policy are available, distribute them. After a few minutes' review, ask participants for the main points of that policy. For question 6, point out that most experts recommend purging after 90 days, but circumstances will dictate appropriate time periods.)

3. Distribute Handout 12.1, "What's Your EQ (Electronic Quotient)? Ask participants to answer the questions and then lead a brief discussion based on the answers: 1. B ("Email: Tool or Torment?" in *Solutions,* Summer 2001, p. 15); 2. C ("When in doubt, delete that e-mail," by Clinton Wilder, www.optimizemag.com, October 2002, p. 84); 3. A (Survey by META Group, Inc. of Stamford, CT; reported by Jupiter Media Corporation [www.internet.com], October 2002); 4. C (Customer Respect Report released by International Ventures Research Limited, October 2002; reported at www.CustomerRespect.com); 5. A (You can verify by visiting such sites as www.HoaxBusters.ciac.org or www.grahamsurbanlegend.tk).

4. Conclude by incorporating the Points of Interest in your reminder that the electronic surfing, sending, and receiving of material not related to work reduce productivity. Further, they may violate internal policy and could cost employees their jobs.

Variation

Icebreaker: Begin the class by distributing the handout. Ask participants to find others who had the same answers they did. (They can form dyads, triads, or small groups. Those who cannot find anyone with an identical set of answers can form a "group" of their own.) Ask which group had answers B, C, D, E, A. Ask them to stand for an ovation from the other participants. Then probe: "Were these lucky guesses or do some of you have some experience with e-mail ethics? If so, can you share that with us now?"

Discussion

➤ Should the regulations set forth in an organization's e-mail policies be strictly enforced?

➤ If so, how should that enforcement be handled?

➤ Should such policies have "zero tolerance"?

> ➤ Do employers have the right to invade employees' electronic privacy? (Discuss in relation to the legal right versus the ethical right of monitoring employees' e-mail communications.)

Quotation

"In the event of a workplace lawsuit, employees' home computers may be reviewed along with the company's computers."
—Nancy Flynn, *The ePolicy Handbook*

Points of Interest

➤ An e-mail circulated by male employees ("25 reasons why beer is better than women") cost a major corporation $2.2 million to settle a sexual harassment lawsuit.

➤ The State of Michigan, Department of Management and Budget, offers these guidelines for the use of computer passwords (reprinted with permission from Office of Administrative Services):

Don't use common words in proper or reverse spelling.

Don't use common computer acronyms.

Don't use names of famous or fictitious people.

Don't use your login name in any form.

Don't use your first, middle, or last name in any form.

Don't use your spouse's or child's name.

Don't use easily obtained numbers such as telephone, street, or social security.

Don't use passwords starting with a digit or composed entirely of digits.

Don't write your password on paper affixed to your desk or PC.

INTERNET AND PRODUCTIVITY

1. What are the main points of your company's Internet/e-mail policy?

2. How much time do you spend each week sending/receiving electronic information that is not directly related to your job?

3. How much time do you think is spent on the Internet by others in your department?

4. Calculate the cost, on an annual basis, of this time.

5. How much regulation is too much regulation?

6. How often should e-files be purged?

What's Your EQ (Electronic Quotient)?

1. How much time does the average executive spend using e-mail?
   A. 20 minutes per day
   B. 2 hours per day
   C. 20 hours per week
   D. 200 hours per year
   E. None of the above

2. According to a recent study by the Radicati Group in Palo Alto, California, what percentage of a person's e-mail is actual spam?
   A. 3%
   B. 13%
   C. 32%
   D. 44%
   E. 51%

3. Experts predict that a majority of companies will spend what percentage of their IT budget on security in 2003?
   A. 5%
   B. 15%
   C. 25%
   D. 35%

4. In a recent survey of Fortune 100 companies, what percentage failed to reply to general inquiries submitted to their Web site?
   A. 3%
   B. 13%
   C. 37%
   D. 53%
   E. None of the above

5. If you wanted to verify the truth of rumors, hoaxes, and urban legends, it's possible to do so electronically.
   A. True
   B. False

13

To Be or Not to Be . . . Civil

Approximately 25 minutes

Overview

This exercise helps participants explore the line (not always a fine one) between the letter of the law and the spirit of the law. It uses a real-world scenario and asks participants to compare it to similar situations they've experienced.

Purpose

To encourage thought and discussion regarding instances when it may be appropriate to break, bend, or ignore the rules that govern a corporate entity.

Group Size

Any number of individuals can participate. The group should be divided into subgroups of four or five.

Room Arrangement

If possible, arrange table groups for four or five participants each.

Materials

➤ Transparency 13.1, *"Discussion Questions"*

➤ Projector for transparencies or for PowerPoint slides

Method

1. Share with the class this true story, as reported by Chicago columnist Mike Royko:

   *Brendan Hodges was a young musician, walking along Chicago streets, minding his own business until a thug made it **his** business to take Brendan's bass guitar. When Brendan tried to hold on to it, the thief shot the young man in the eye. Although the boy was attended by some of the city's best doctors at Cook County Hospital, his parents, Michael and Miriam Hodges, were told when they arrived that the boy might not make it.*

Immediately after meeting with the physicians, they rushed to an elevator, anxious to be at their son's bedside. The operator, though, informed them that they both needed visitors' passes. Understandably agitated, Mr. Hodges told the operator that their son was dying, hoping the urgency of the situation would settle the matter. Instead, the elevator operator accused Brendan's parents of having an "attitude." He then called for security.

Wanting to avoid further delay and a confrontation with security, Mr. Hodges attempted to get the elevator moving up to his son's floor but found the doors wouldn't close, even though he had pressed the floor button. At this point, security officers arrived, pushed Mrs. Hodges to the side, and actually handcuffed her husband. They then led him off to their office, where he was forced to wait until the security lieutenant arrived. The lieutenant chastised the grieving father: **"We have rules and regulations,"** *he informed him,* **"and if we let you get away with it, we'd have to let everyone get away with it."**

The officer, who had apparently received an erroneous update from someone else, charged, **"You've been clowning around here since 11:00 this morning."** *Mr. Hodges responded by pointing out that coming to the hospital to be with a dying child could hardly be termed "clowning around." He was finally released, but precious time had been lost. Brendan Hodges died the next morning.*

2. Ask small groups to discuss the questions shown on Transparency 13.1, *"Discussion Questions,"* for 15 or 20 minutes.

3. Have a spokesperson from each group deliver a brief summary.

4. Close with reference to a nationally publicized incident of subordinates questioning leaders. Cite as examples Coleen Rowley, FBI agent in the Minnesota field office, and Sherron Watkins, vice president of Enron Corporation. Each of them went out on a professional limb and voiced their concerns about practices in which their superiors were engaged. Leaders are simply not always right, as shown in the example of Jim Jones, who "led" hundreds of people to their collective suicidal deaths.

Variation

Related Programs: In leadership programs especially, the idea of challenging the leader instead of following him or her without question is worthy of exploration. Not only should leaders expect empowered subordinates to challenge, question, and even "blow the whistle," but they should also welcome inquiries designed to ensure progress is being made, and made in the right direction.

Discussion

➤ How can we develop the sensitivity required for situations involving raw human emotion?

➤ What immediate and far-reaching benefits might ensue from such development?

➤ How can an organization encourage rule enforcement and simultaneously encourage the occasional flouting of rules?

Quotation

"So many gods, so many creeds,
So many paths that wind and wind, While just the art of being
*   kind is all the sad world needs."*
—Ella Wheeler Wilcox, poet (1850–1919)

Points of Interest

In their research on workplace incivility ("Assessing and Attacking Workplace Incivility," authors Christine Pearson, Lynne Andersson, and Christine Porath of the University of North Carolina at Chapel Hill cite a recent national poll in which 90 percent of respondents regarded incivility as a serious problem, one that leads to violence and the erosion of moral values. Their research appears in a forthcoming book, *Organizational Dynamics,* a publication of the American Management Association.

DISCUSSION QUESTIONS

1. What rules (policies, regulations, laws) should never be broken?

2. Which should or could be bent?

3. On what occasions?

4. Can you teach good judgment to others? If so, how?

5. How often are your organization's rules revisited or revised?

14 Librarians Don't Rule the World!

Approximately 15 minutes

Overview

Ethics "training" begins with ethics awareness. This exercise brings forth such awareness via pictorial images, which are then related to the corporate culture.

Purpose

To develop ethics awareness via imaginative depictions.

Group Size

The group can be of any size. Participants will first work alone and then in triads.

Room Arrangement

No special arrangements are required.

Materials

➤ One magic marker, crayon, or colored pencil for each participant
➤ One sheet of paper for each participant

Method

1. Begin with a dramatic flourish. Announce: *"Some of you may think that knowledge is power. [Pause.] You're wrong. Knowledge is **not** power. If it were, librarians would rule the world. And, we all know they don't! Einstein himself said that 'imagination is more important than knowledge.' And the venerable Tom Peters has declared, 'Imagination is the only source of real value in the new economy.'*

   "This activity will test your imaginative powers. It asks you to take 5 minutes and come up with a pictorial image of your

organization's ethical climate. Do not use any words at all—just images to represent the morality level where you work. Think about your culture and what principles define it. Then, translate that definition or description into a visual image. You have 5 minutes. Please get started now."

2. Next, ask participants to form triads and to share their images and the meanings behind them.

3. Ask for volunteers to share their imaginative insights. If the images of the ethical climate were negative, try to uncover the causes of the problem. When the images reflect a positive moral climate, ask what the driving forces behind that reflection are.

4. Finally, lead a discussion that might provide new, improved, enhanced perceptions (and realities) of the ethical climate within participants' organizations. Segue from the causes to possible cures in relation to the negative images. For the positive images, suggest possible extensions of the driving forces to some of the negative descriptions or situations.

Variation

Collect the unsigned depictions. Mount them on a wall and invite someone outside the training room (ideally, a member of senior management) to select the one he or she feels most accurately depicts the existing corporate climate as far as ethics are concerned.

Discussion

➤ If yours were an ideal ethical climate, what visual image would you use to represent it?

➤ What steps can or should be taken to move from the real to the ideal?

➤ Is there a discrepancy between the Values or Ethics Statement issued by senior management and the perceptions held by the rank and file?

➤ If so, how can the gap be closed?

Quotation

"Clay is molded to make a vessel, but the utility of the vessel lies in the space where there is nothing. Thus, taking advantage of what is, we recognize the utility of what is not."
—Lao Tzu, philosopher (circa 600 B.C.E.)

**Points
of Interest**

When the metaphorical vessel of trust has been cracked, leaders
must work very hard to make it whole again. That trust can be
regained, in time, via good, honest meetings that restore
confidence in an organization that may have been tainted by
ethical missteps or mistakes. Author Mark McMaster, writing in
Successful Meetings ("Let the Healing Begin," October 2002, p.
67), recommends that senior management be involved in these
meetings. He also advises leaders to encourage dialog, to include
everyone, and to create a comfortable forum in which issues can
be discussed.

ETHICAL WORKPLACE CONDUCT

Everybody Does It 15

Lloyd A. Conway

Approximately 20 minutes

Overview

This exercise presents five all-too-familiar workplace scenarios and challenges participants to explore the ramifications of all-too-familiar reactions to those scenarios.

Purpose

To encourage more ethical behavior with regard to little things, which, when considered as a totality, are immensely costly for the organization.

Group Size

Any number of participants can work on this exercise, which initially involves individual work and then small group discussions.

Room Arrangement

No special arrangements are required other than seating that permits seats to be rearranged to form small groups.

Materials

Handout 15.1, *"Everybody Does It"*

Procedure

1. Lead a discussion of "cognitive dissonance," a psychological term that refers to ways we justify information that runs contrary to our values. For example, we all know it's wrong to steal, but many of us would be willing to take company tape or clips or paper for our own use. To resolve the dissonance that results from doing something we know is wrong, we might say to ourselves, *"It only costs a penny,"* or *"They'll never miss it,"* or *"This is a small compensation for the pay*

raise I didn't get." (Worse yet, some would not even feel the dissonance: they simply take the item without even thinking about it.)

2. Ask for other examples from the national scene: How do Democrats, for example, resolve the dissonance caused by having the President involved in a scandal? How do anti-war Republicans support a pro-war President?

3. Explain that you'd like to explore the issue further via workplace examples.

4. Distribute Handout 15.1, *"Everybody Does It,"* and allow about 15 minutes for completion.

5. Form small groups and have participants share their responses.

6. Bring closure to the exercise by asking for a spokesperson from each group to present a synopsis of the discussion.

Variation

Ask for a volunteer to calculate the potential cost of each scenario by:

1. Passing out small sheets of paper after the first scenario and asking each participant to indicate anonymously whether or not he or she has used the company's fax machine or copy machine for his or her own purposes.

2. Calculating the percentage of people, compared to the class total, who do employ company property for their own use. On the same sheet, ask each person to indicate the number of times in a given year that he or she uses the company fax machine or copy machine for personal use.

3. Calculating the cost of such action in terms of lost productivity.

4. Multiplying that cost times the number of times it is likely to happen in a given year for a single employee.

5. Multiplying that cost times the number of employees in the organization.

6. Multiplying that cost by the percentage of employees who are likely to engage in such conduct based on the percentage you came up with from step 2.

Discussion

➤ What characteristics will business leaders need for success a decade from now?

➤ What are some of the reasons people give for small violations of ethics?

➤ Is it worth a manager's time to attempt to put an end to such violations?

➤ Assume you are the head of the department or head of the company. What would you say to end such "conversion thefts"?

Quotation

"Anything you do is everything you do."
—Buddhist saying

Points of Interest

"Profitability and the Common Good," an article by Pam Mayer, reports an interesting study from the Johnson School of Management at Cornell University. The School surveyed executives from several Fortune 1000 companies and asked, *"What characteristics will business leaders need for success a decade from now?"* The top two answers from these executives were **team-building** and **compassion.** These two elements would easily appear on a list of traits possessed by ethical leaders. It's reassuring to find, at least in this study, that today's executives are concerned with the common good.

By comparison, the same question was asked of MBA students from the top 20 business schools. Their responses related to profitability: the trait they selected was an orientation toward results. (Only 28 percent of the students strongly agreed that corporations have a responsibility to the environment. Half the executives were in strong agreement with the statement.)

"Everybody Does It"

DIRECTIONS

We all realize that a clerk taking money from the cash register is stealing; that the Enron and Global Crossing scandals, in which insider information was used for personal profit and to mislead the public, are morally wrong. But in the commonplace occurrences of our everyday lives, do we stop to think about the small ways in which our integrity is put to the test? Read each of these scenarios and answer the questions related to them as honestly as possible.

1. Your child's school calls you at work, because you forgot to turn in a signed permission slip for today's field trip. The school secretary offers to fax you one to sign; your return of the signed paper will permit your child to join his classmates. If not, a sad face will greet you after a day of being left behind at school, while everyone else had a great time.

   What do you do?

   _____

   What is your employer's policy on personal fax use?

   _____

   Would it be different if the fax involved a long-distance call? Why or why not?

   _____

   _____

   Would the situation be different if the fax were for a car loan application, student loan paperwork, or an RSVP to a retirement dinner? If so, tell how, in reference to each of these three situations.

   _____

   _____

   _____

_____

_____

_____

_____

2. You're responsible for making flyers for the PTA bake sale. Would you copy them on the company copier? If so, what would your rationale be?

_____

_____

_____

_____

What is your employer's policy on personal use of the copier?

_____

Would it matter if you brought your own paper?

_____

Would it matter if it were for a charity, as opposed to something for private gain, such as "For Sale" flyers for your used computer?

_____

3. Most employers have policies covering local phone calls. If yours does, do they limit the times when calls can be made or accepted? If local calls are acceptable, is there an issue with the amount of time spent on the phone, as opposed to phone charges? Share your views here of what is or, perhaps, what should be allowed.

_____

_____

_____

_____

_____

(continued)

4. Think of a scenario involving actions that might be described as being in a "gray zone." The scenario could be related to checking personal e-mail while at work, using the Internet to shop or bank online, favoring a friend in a hiring or promotion situation, or something similar. Tell the consequences of these actions, specifying, if you can, how "innocent" things can lead to trouble (gossip, damaged reputations, reprimands, etc.).

_____

_____

_____

_____

5. What overall conclusions can be drawn about habits and the "everybody does it" syndrome at work?

_____

_____

_____

_____

The fancy legal term for much of the preceding is "theft by conversion," or using someone else's property without asking for permission in order to meet your own needs. Even if you don't agree that all of the examples given in the preceding are wrong, ask yourself how you would react if you read in the newspaper that employees of your children's school or the City Hall were engaged in such actions and getting paid with your tax dollars. Remember, it's what we do when no one is looking that truly shows our character (and in the digital age, somebody is probably looking).

ETHICAL WORKPLACE CONDUCT

Flirting with Danger

Eve Strella and Gwen Martone

Approximately 60 to 75 minutes

Overview

Participants are encouraged to think about the ethical ramifications of seemingly innocent acts, such as flirtatious behaviors, sexual innuendoes, seductive remarks, and/or invitations.

Purpose

To make participants aware of personal and organizational liabilities that follow certain actions.

Group Size

The ideal group size would be 18 to 20 participants, subdivided into groups of four or five.

Room Arrangement

If possible, arrange table groups serving as four separate workstations.

Materials

➤ Projector for transparencies or for PowerPoint slides
➤ Transparency 16.1, *"Gender Dynamics in the Workplace"*
➤ Transparency 16.2, *"Definition: Gender Dynamics"*
➤ Transparency 16.3, *"Definition: Boundary"*
➤ Bright-colored Post-it® notes
➤ Masking tape

➤ Flipchart with the following headings written at the top of the first three pages:

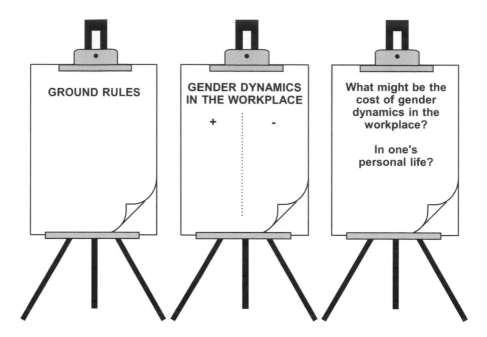

GROUND RULES

GENDER DYNAMICS IN THE WORKPLACE

+ | -

What might be the cost of gender dynamics in the workplace?

In one's personal life?

Procedure

1. Have Transparency 16.1, *"Gender Dynamics in the Workplace,"* on the screen. Introduce the general topic of interpersonal dynamics and transition to the more specific topic of gender dynamics and how they may impede workplace harmony and productivity. Ask for (and/or provide) a few short examples such as "flirtatious behaviors," "sexual innuendoes," "seductive remarks," "unsolicited hugs."

2. Turn to the **Ground Rules** page on the flipchart. List your expectations of participants and ask them to share their expectations of you.

3. Ask the group to define "gender dynamics." Following a brief discussion, offer the definition that appears on Transparency 16.2, *"Definition of Gender Dynamics."*

4. Ask small groups to discuss the topic by exploring both the positive and negative consequences of this form of energy in a workplace setting. One spokesperson per group will then verbalize the group discussion and write the key points on the second flipchart page titled "Gender Dynamics in the Workplace."

5. On separate Post-it® notes, each participant will list five behaviors he or she engages in, or perhaps has been invited to engage in, at work. Ask for volunteers to share their lists and then ask that they be posted on the wall or on a new flipchart page.

6. Lead a large-group discussion using the Post-it® notes on the wall or flipchart. Focus on the possible negative consequences that might result from the behaviors listed. Elicit examples of such from participants—for example, someone may have been at a meeting when a colleague made an unsolicited, inappropriate gesture or made a remark tinged with sexist language.

7. Turn to the third flipchart page next and continue the discussion by noting answers to the question written at the top: **What might be the cost of gender dynamics in the workplace?** Concentrate on the negative outcomes such as the million-dollar lawsuits won by women who were forced to work in a hostile environment.

8. Conclude by facilitating a large-group discussion regarding the importance of having healthy boundaries in workplace environments. Ask what a boundary is. Show Transparency 16.3, *"Definition: Boundary,"* and share this definition of a "boundary" in gender-dynamics terms: *"It's an understanding of where you and another person begin and end; it's the specification of a limit, personally and professionally."*

9. Raise these questions as well: *"Would you entertain these behaviors* (identified in 5) *in the presence of your or the other person's significant other?" "Would you entertain them in the presence of other work colleagues?"*

10. Point out that what you *truthfully* recognize as a gray area or an area of "danger" is an area in which you are likely to transgress boundaries. Encourage participants to follow this process of thinking about costs and questions and boundaries the next time, and every time, they encounter gray areas.

Variation

Work to devise other questions for other aspects of the work environment. For example, when considering what customers expect, want, or deserve, ask, "If the customer could see what I'm doing right now, would the customer be willing to pay for it?" When wondering if a given action is something that falls within the boundaries of ethical leadership, the question might be, "If this action were to appear as a headline in tomorrow's newspaper, would I still proceed with it?"

Discussion

➤ What's the most efficient way to enhance creative energy while maintaining healthy collegial boundaries?

➤ Should these boundaries be monitored? If so, how? Should policies be created regarding such boundaries?

➤ Do employers have the right to address sexually energized behaviors in the workplace?

➤ Where does the workplace environment begin and end?

Quotation

"To love is to admire with the heart; to admire is to love with the mind."
—Theophile Gautier

Points of Interest

As illustrated in *Successful Meetings,* an inappropriate illustration of gender dynamics cost a top Fox Television executive his job. In a prepared speech delivered to a conference of 200 executives in Snowmass, Colorado, in June, 1992, Stephen Chao wanted to make the point that violence was more obscene than nudity and sexuality. As planned, a young man whom Chao had hired appeared beside the speaker, completely naked. Immediately after his presentation, Chao was confronted by Rupert Murdoch, who fired him on the spot. As Murdoch later explained, *"There's one thing this company must make clear—that there are limits."*

ILLUMINATE OF ROCHESTER, INC., is a coaching, consulting, training, and team development organization whose focus is to assist individuals and organizations in transition through issues of change, layoffs, mergers, abusive management and co-worker behavior, and fear in the workplace. Co-CEOs Eve Strella and Gwen Martone have merged their expertise as an industrial engineer and a clinical therapist with a combined 32 years of hands-on experience in the area of human solutions.

GENDER DYNAMICS IN THE WORKPLACE

DEFINITION:
GENDER DYNAMICS

Refers to the energy exchanged between members of the same or opposite sex. These exchanges are often charged with some degree of tension, however slight, and are usually characterized as flirtatious in nature.

DEFINITION: BOUNDARY

An understanding of where you and another person begin and end; the specification of a limit, personally and professionally.

17 Leader of the PAC

Approximately 45 minutes

Overview

Participants in this exercise, based on an actual corporate practice, answer a series of questions related to a new-hire situation. Then they discuss the pros and cons of a particular course of action.

Purpose

To provide alternatives to actions that may be troublesome.

Group Size

Any number of individuals can work on this exercise but there should be an even number of subgroups.

Room Arrangement

No special arrangements are required.

Materials

Handout 17.1, *"Leader of the PAC"*

Procedure

1. Ask the group members what they know and how they feel about campaign contributions in general and those made by businesses or businesspeople in particular. Bring into the discussion some ethical issues raised by such contributions.

2. Distribute Handout 17.1, *"Leader of the PAC,"* and ask participants to answer the questions on the bottom.

3. After about 15 minutes, have participants form small groups to prepare a script that has a newly hired employee actually explain to his or her manager that he or she prefers not to participate in the program.

4. Have each group present to one other group and obtain feedback on the effectiveness of the scripted presentation.

Then the second group will make its presentation to the group that has just presented and will receive feedback from them. (**Note:** If there is an odd number of groups, have the "odd" group present to the entire class and then meet with you in a breakout room or a corner of the classroom. If the other groups are still working after you've provided feedback, split your group up; each person will join a different group and sit in as an observer.)

5. Lead a discussion about the need to speak up for what one believes is right juxtaposed with the need to be realistic in an "office politics" setting.

6. Conclude by challenging participants to come up with an original three- or four-word phrase that simply inspires. (Examples could be "Never give up," "Just do it," and "Just say no.") Post their declarations around the room.

Variation

To illustrate the delicate balance required as managers walk the corporate tightrope, instead of having all the groups write an employee-centered script, have only half do this. The other half will write the script from the viewpoint of a manager who's been told by his or her own manager that his or her performance appraisal depends, in part, on the amount of money contributed by his or her department to Political Action Committees. They should assume the manager sees nothing wrong with campaign contributions, as he or she honestly believes they help protect jobs.

Discussion

➤ Why do you think there's been so much resistance to campaign reform?

➤ Will efforts to influence political leaders disappear now that reform is official? Explain your answer. Draw a line in the middle of a sheet of paper. List on the left all the reasons why a new hire might hesitate to express his or her opposition to such contributions. On the right, list all the reasons why he or she might "go along to get along."

Quotation

"There may be times when we are powerless to prevent injustice, but there must never be a time when we fail to protest."
—Elie Wiesel

**Points
of Interest**

The McCain–Feingold Campaign Finance Reform Bill, passed by Congress in March 2002, was propelled by people such as Russell Feingold, who feel that the overhaul of campaign finance was sorely needed. Feingold has publicly referred to soft money as a "taint" on the democracy. "Soft money" refers to the no-holds-barred contributions wealthy individuals, corporations, and labor unions can make to political parties. In theory, such money cannot be used for campaigning in federal elections. In reality, prior to the passage of new legislation targeting soft money, it was used primarily for federal elections.

Leader of the PAC

You are the successful candidate (the final "short list" had 12 contenders) for a job that you've dreamed of all your life. It's your first day now with a company that leases buildings to the federal government. As you're settling in, your supervisor approaches, shakes your hand, and then gives you the following letter:

> The Rogert Employee Political Action Committee (REPAC) welcomes you to our organization. As you may know, only administrative, executive, managerial, and professional personnel, like yourself, who are earning more than $70,000 annually are invited to participate in REPAC.
>
> Of course, Rogert, Inc., does not show favoritism toward those who do not join REPAC. Nor do we consider the amount contributed when promotional decisions are made and/or career opportunities are extended. The program is entirely voluntary. However, it is important to know that our dollars have helped protect property-management jobs: to date, every single one of our buildings has at least two government tenants leasing a minimum of 90,000 square feet of space.
>
> Please call us if you have questions. Your assistance and cooperation are appreciated. Know that Rogert senior management remains committed to involving key people in the political process. That process is paramount to our people and their jobs.

1. What sentences, if any, do you find troublesome?

   _____

   _____

   _____

2. What questions does this letter evoke?

   _____

   _____

   _____

(continued)

3. Would you be likely to call the person who wrote this letter to get answers to those questions? Why or why not?

_____

_____

_____

4. Would you join REPAC? Explain your decision.

_____

_____

_____

5. Would you make a donation? If not, why not? If so, why and how much?

_____

_____

_____

Additional comments:

_____

_____

_____

_____

_____

_____

ETHICAL WORKPLACE CONDUCT

Lobbying for Positions

Approximately 15 minutes

Overview	This exercise asks participants to design an ethics-based question that might help job applicants self-screen before making important decisions.
Purpose	➤ To identify the "irreducible essence" of a company. ➤ To help participants clarify values.
Group Size	Any number of individuals can participate. The group should be divided into subgroups of three or four participants each.
Room Arrangement	No special arrangements are required.
Materials	➤ Flipchart ➤ Marking pens
Procedure	1. Introduce the exercise by writing on the flipchart: "Do you believe America should be building weapons of mass destruction? If not, you shouldn't be applying for a job with this company." Explain that, according to one urban legend, a large West Coast defense contractor has this sign prominently displayed in its lobby, right outside the entrance to the Human Resources department, where applicants would have to go to be interviewed. From the get-go, the company wants prospective employees to be fully aware of what the company

does. They realize that if applicants feel the company product is immoral, they simply should not be considering employment there.

2. Ask participants to consider what Senator Hubert Humphrey referred to as an "irreducible essence," that is, when all else is stripped away, what is your fundamental core, your basic essence, the unshakeable element that remains? For Humphrey, it was love of country. For individuals and organizations alike, the essence question is an important one to ask. Elicit a few responses from participants or perhaps provide your own.

3. Now have participants think about what it is their organization stands for or does. (If the group has several people who work in the same organization, they may wish to work together on this question.)

4. Once they've determined their organization's *raison d'être,* task them with asking a question and then supplying an answer similar to the one described in step 1.

5. Have small groups discuss whether the essence question (and answer) conflicts with their personal values. If so, invite them to discuss what, if anything, they intend to do about this potential conflict in values.

Variation

Invite participants to consider what it is they stand for—as men, women, employees, managers, team members, Americans, et cetera. Have them draft a letter sharing what they've learned over the years about values in a workplace setting. The recipient of the letter is a hypothetical new employee.

Urge the person responsible for new-employee orientation to include some of these letters in the orientation brochure.

Discussion

➤ How much congruence exists between what you value and what your organization, department, or department head values? If a gap exists, how troubled are you by it?

➤ How widely disseminated are your organization's values?

➤ Other than the need to earn a paycheck, what keeps people in places that don't reflect their personally held values?

Quotation

"The palest ink is better than the best memory."
—Chinese proverb

**Points
of Interest**

When there's a lack of congruence between a company's public statements and its private practice, everyone suffers. Such was the case with Wal-Mart's "Made Right Here" proclamation, as reported by Keri Hayes. Along with 17 other companies, Wal-Mart was named in a class-action lawsuit, filed on behalf of 50,000 employees in Saipan (where, according to a Department of Interior spokesman, pregnant women were coerced to have abortions or to lose their jobs). The National Labor Committee found that 85 percent of Wal-Mart's private-label merchandise was not "made right here," but rather was manufactured in other countries.

19 Neutron Neutrality

Approximately 25 minutes

Overview

Based on an article regarding a suicide attributed to job loss, this exercise asks participants to consider ways to make job loss less negative and more neutral, if not positive.

Purpose

To engender creative ideas for making job loss less traumatic.

Group Size

Any number of individuals can participate. Participants will first work alone and then in subgroups of four or five.

Room Arrangement

No special arrangement are required other than seating flexible enough to permit small-group formations.

Materials

Handout 19.1, *"Termination Facts"*; articles about Jack Welch obtained or downloaded in advance of class

Method

1. Start the exercise by asking if anyone has read *Straight from the Gut,* the biography of General Electric's (GE) former CEO, Jack Welch. Engage the group in a brief discussion about Welch and some of the policies he's instituted at General Electric (such as the Work-Out). Also have them discuss some of the remarks for which he's famous ("When the rate of change outside the company is greater than the rate of change inside the company, then we are looking at the beginning of the end"). Note that while he's been called the Manager of the Century, he's also been called Neutron Jack, for policies that leave buildings standing but people decimated.

2. Explain that one of those policies—to cut costs whenever and wherever possible—is highlighted in their handout. Ask participants to read the facts related to GE's termination procedure at Erie Works and then to answer the questions on the handout.

3. Distribute Handout 19.1, *"Termination Facts,"* and ask everyone to work on it individually.

4. Then have participants work in groups of four or five to come up with at least five ways to make terminations less painful. Encourage full use of their creative talents as they consider suicide-preventive measures as well as supportive overtures the organization can extend to laid off workers.

5. Have a reporter from each group write the group's ideas on flipchart paper, to be posted around the room.

6. Bring closure by asking, "How many of you have lost a job at least once in your life?" "How many feel that subsequent jobs were even better than the one you lost?" "How can this information be shared with employees who face termination?" Have a scribe record the ideas and add them to the ideas listed in the preceding step.

7. Ask for a volunteer to disseminate the ideas to anyone within the organization who has responsibility for advising employees they are being terminated.

Variation

Adapt the Work-Out session to a training situation in the following way.

1. Explore the many benefits of Work-Out session; for example, they encourage employees to take the work out of work. On another level, the sessions help employees work out their problems. In addition, the sessions, like their aerobic counterparts, make the organization leaner and stronger. They also allow senior management to learn more about lower-level employees and the contributions they can make.

2. Choose issue(s) to discuss.

3. Select a cross-functional team appropriate for the problem.

4. Choose a champion who will help recommendations become reality.

5. Let the team meet for 3 days (or as needed) to draw up recommendations for improving processes.

6. Meet with the manager who must respond with "yes," "no," or "maybe" to recommendations on the spot. Reasons and details are provided for each decision.

7. Hold additional meetings as needed to pursue recommendations.

8. Continue the process with these and other issues.

These steps, adapted for the classroom learning situation, involve groups working in teams and observers noting their interactions.

1. Select four observers and instruct them as follows: "Four of you will serve as observers—one for each of the reporting teams. Your first assignment is to observe the interactions among the teams attempting to find solutions for the owner's problem. The team should come up with at least five possibilities. Look for interpersonal and group dynamics examples of:

Positive Behaviors	Negative Behaviors
Leadership	Domination of the discussion
Creativity	Belittling remarks
Harmony	Poor listening
Full participation	Side conversations

"As soon as the team has prepared a list of suggestions and solutions, share your observations with them."

"Your second assignment requires you to observe the 'owner's' reaction to the team's suggestions. Did he or she, for example, take notes? Was he or she defensive? Did he or she give realistic responses? What did you learn about the 'problem-owner' by watching his or her responses to the suggestions of the team? After the Work-Out session is concluded, you will meet with the 'owner' privately and share your observations with him or her."

2. Next, divide the group into four subgroups. Then, each person in each subgroup will quickly name (but not discuss) a solvable work-related problem. The problem each group ultimately selects should be one that—once solved or resolved—will help the "problem-owner" achieve some measure of success in coping with this problem or issue. It should also be a problem that is solvable and one that will have benefit to the organization.

3. Give this instruction: "As you listen to your group members, don't offer solutions to the problems you hear described. Instead, allow each person to state the problem so that it is clearly understood by the others in the group. Questions are allowed, but only for the purpose of clarification, not for solution-seeking.

4. "Then, as a group, select the one problem that most needs attention. The 'owner' of the problem will present it to another group and will then leave the room while the group to which the problem was presented discusses feasible solutions. (Observers will note the extent of positive and negative interpersonal exchanges.) Your group will work to find five or more possible solutions for the problem that the 'problem-owner' presented to you.

5. "When the 'owner' returns, your group will present its suggested solutions. The 'owner' must immediately decide to accept (with a rationale), reject (with reasons), or table (with an explanation of why and when) each of the solutions. An observing team (represented by senior management in the real world) later meets with the 'owner'.

6. "Four 'owners' will read articles about the GE Work-Outs and will have a 5- to 10-minute report ready. The report will describe Work-Outs in greater detail and the benefits they're designed to create. The report will be given at the end of the Work-Out session.

Discussion

➤ What other public figures can you recall who are highly regarded despite what many consider serious flaws?

➤ What lies behind people's willingness to regard such people so highly?

➤ What does it say about our national tolerance for unethical behavior when we read lists such as the one that appears in the Points of Interest?

Quotation

"A mind all logic is like a knife all blade. It makes the hand bleed that uses it."
—Rabindranath Tagore

Points of Interest

New words are constantly being added to our vocabulary of 1,000,000+ words. Sometimes, old words or phrases are given new meaning. Such is the case with "low-hanging fruit," a Work-Out associated word that encourages group members to dispense quickly with issues that are so easy to deal with they can be quickly "plucked off." (These issues, ironically, often consume a great deal of time and are popular sources of complaints.)

These "fruit" issues can be discussed as well in programs that deal with stress, time management, productivity, leadership, interpersonal skills, et cetera.

Termination Facts

DIRECTIONS

Read these facts, excerpted from an article by Thomas O'Boyle ("Profit at Any Cost." *Business Ethics,* March/April 1999, pp. 13–14). Then answer the questions that follow.

➤ At Erie Works, a General Electric (GE) site, Ivan Winebrenner, age 39, received a termination notice on June 10, 1993. He was one of 200 from the Erie Works plants who were let go because of "lack of work."

➤ Two days later, his wife found him dead in their bedroom from a gunshot wound to the head.

➤ Two days after this discovery, co-worker Anthony Victor Torelli turned a gun on himself, having failed to find his foreman at the plant. There have been several suicides since among the ranks of the Erie Works plant.

➤ The engineering supervisor at the plant, Sheldon Potter, who quit rather than participate in the layoffs, describes the process as "totally inhuman in any other context." (The "inhuman" label came about for many reasons. To illustrate, GE has a practice of routinely eliminating the lower 10% of managers whose performance appraisals are less stellar than the appraisals of their peers. Welch, many say, moved the company from paternalism to cannibalism by, for example, closing or selling 98 plants, even though—as was the case with Erie Works—dedicated employees were working hard to increase profitability. Whistleblowers were dismissed rather than applauded for bring ethical violations to management's attention.)

➤ Employees at this GE site were given laminated cards with a statement of GE's Beliefs—the first of which is "People, working together, are the source of our strength."

➤ In the year when the suicides occurred, Erie Works had recorded its best profits ever.

(continued)

➤ The layoffs were the result of a corporate decision to convert the manufacture of locomotive parts from an in-house production to the purchase of these parts from an outside vendor.

➤ GE's former CEO moved the company from eleventh in stock value among American corporations to first place.

➤ In the streamlining process, 300,000 people lost their jobs.

How humane do you feel your company's termination policy is?

If you were a CEO, driven to produce profits for shareholders and other stakeholders, what would your top priority be?

Is it unethical for an organization to engage in cost-cutting—even if it means job loss?

How can the termination process be made more humane?

ETHICAL WORKPLACE CONDUCT

Whatever It Takes

Approximately 25 minutes

Overview

For participants who have been caught between company loyalty and a private morality, this exercise, based on an actual event, illustrates the difficulty and possible consequences of "doing the right thing." For those who have not yet had that experience, the exercise affords an opportunity for advance preparation.

Purpose

➤ To explore the ramifications of defying a manager's suggestion.

➤ To provide ideas for achieving clarity regarding job expectations.

Group Size

Any number of individuals can participate. The group should be divided into subgroups of four or five.

Room Arrangement

No special arrangements are required other than seating flexible enough to permit small groups to be formed.

Materials

➤ Flipchart

➤ Marking pens

➤ Handout 20.1, *"Checklist"*

➤ Handout 20.2, *"Whatever It Takes"*

Procedure

1. Ask participants to complete Handout 20.1 and to share some of their answers with a partner.

2. Lead into the next part of the exercise by alluding to some of the questions on the checklist and noting that a lack of communication or poor communication can lead us into difficult or confusing positions. Usually, because of our background and experience, we're able to handle those challenges with no adverse repercussions. (In truth, we sometimes emerge from those conflicts stronger than we were before encountering them.) Other times, though, the lack of clarity could lead to dangerous or expensive results.

3. Use examples that range from the micro- to the macrocosmic. For example, a simple, two-letter pronoun can leave a reader or listener wondering what was meant, as shown in this sentence: "Tom showed his supervisor the report *he* had written 3 years earlier."

   A more serious situation involves J. Edgar Hoover, legendary head of FBI, who was apparently a stickler for details. On a sloppily written report that had been submitted to him regarding immigration problems, he wrote "Watch the borders!" While he simply meant the margins on the paper were not uniform, the report-writer interpreted the comment to mean additional funds should be spent patrolling the international borders and proceeded to publish his interpretation.

4. Then ask participants to reflect on similar situations they've experienced, situations in which poorly worded communications led to misunderstandings or perhaps even to ethical or legal violations. In groups of four or five, have them share those experiences.

5. Distribute Handout 20.2 and have the same groups read and discuss the case study.

6. Wrap up the exercise by asking for input from each group. This input will correlate one sentence from the checklist with answers to one of the questions on the case-study handout. For example, if the answer to Question 1 were something akin to, "I would have refused to do what the client was proposing," the Checklist correlation might be, "I'm cognizant of the inherent dangers of my job." If the answer to the same question were, "I would have gone. I know I can handle myself in any situation," the correlation from the Checklist might be, "The training I receive is based on an assessment of my strengths and weaknesses. In a class on assertiveness training, I learned to anticipate trouble and to take

anticipatory action. So I would have called my boss from the client's room (in front of the client) and asked my boss to call me back in 20 minutes to learn the outcome of the deal-making."

Variation

Elicit other difficult scenarios. Record them on the flipchart and assign one to each small group. They'll develop role-plays based on them. After each is enacted, elicit feedback from the whole group regarding lines that were especially effective. Write these on the flip chart and encourage participants to make use of them in the future.

Discussion

➤ Have you given conscious thought to the boundaries you won't cross—no matter what the consequences?

➤ What are some of the unspoken expectations associated with your job—both your expectations and your manager's?

➤ In what circumstances were your principles compromised?

➤ What other situations do you know of in which someone's principles were compromised? What was the result of this compromise?

Quotation

"We are all born originals. Why is it so many of us die copies?"
—Edward Young

Points of Interest

Sometimes people are deliberately vague in their communications, hoping to make a point through vague and veiled wording. This way, they cannot be accused of having deliberately suggested wrongdoing. Ethics author Nan DeMars, writing in *You Want Me To Do* What?, suggest this for ambiguous situations: Restate your understanding of what you're being asked to do, to make certain that you heard what you think you heard. If the implication (or even the expressed request) borders on the illegal or immoral, ask the person who made the request to put it in writing and to sign the written request. If he or she refuses to do so, make a note of the incident and keep it on file. If it's truly an egregious request, request a meeting with a higher authority.

**Points
of Interest**

In the case of *Pullum v. Hudson Foods Inc.,* 871 S.W. 2d 94
(Missouri), Pullum was engaged in horseplay when she should
have been working. Company policy clearly forbids such actions.
When a co-worker threw something at her, Pullum retaliated and
was injured in the process. She sued for compensation benefits,
which the company sought to deny, stating that she was
engaged in an activity that was expressly forbidden.

The courts awarded Pullum compensation benefits, asserting
that her foolish and negligent behavior was irrelevant in light of
the injuries sustained.

Checklist

YES	NO	
❏	❏	I meet regularly with my manager to discuss my career path.
❏	❏	I am fully aware of organizational policies.
❏	❏	My manager and I have discussed the worst mistake I could possibly make as far as this job is concerned.
❏	❏	I know what my manager values.
❏	❏	I'm cognizant of the inherent dangers of my job.
❏	❏	I regularly consider worst-case scenarios related to my job and have appropriate courses of action ready.
❏	❏	I could prioritize the organization's top five values.
❏	❏	The training I receive is based on an assessment of my strengths and weaknesses.
❏	❏	The things I have learned about this organization since being hired lead me to respect it more than I originally did.
❏	❏	I could easily nominate my organization as one of the best 100 American organizations.
❏	❏	Expectations are clearly stated here.
❏	❏	My manager shares information with his or her staff regularly.

Whatever It Takes

THE SITUATION

Pam is a confident, self-assured young woman, a former model who
"retired" from that career at age 30 to enter the world of sales. She's
been moderately successful selling business systems to corporations
and is now having a business dinner in the dining room of a four-star
hotel. The meeting is going well until the prospective buyer suggests
they go up to his room for an after-dinner drink. She demurs, but the
client becomes insistent—going so far as to suggest the six-digit sale is
dependent on an affirmative answer.

"You think about it while I go to the men's room," he tells her and
then excuses himself from the table. Pam immediately calls her boss on
his cell phone and reports the dilemma. His advice: "Do whatever it
takes to get that sale."

1. Had you been Pam, what would you have done?

   _____

   _____

   _____

   _____

2. What are some possible consequences of the different choices Pam
   could have made?

   _____

   _____

   _____

   _____

3. How much clarity is there, on your part and your manager's, regarding job expectations? When was the last time the two of you met to discuss those (changing) expectations?

_____

_____

_____

_____

4. What do you know now about your job that you wish you had known then (when you were first hired)?

_____

_____

_____

_____

Ethical Salesmanship

Ethical Salesmanship

ROBIN WILSON

"Greatness is not found in possessions, power, position or prestige. It is discovered in goodness, humility, service, and character."

—William Mead

The desire to acquire possessions and to secure a new position or greater power often puts blinders on a person's eyes. We live in a society with the attitude that "more is better," driving some people temporarily to set aside their ethics and values. Salespeople will overpromise and yet underdeliver in their quest for a big job or a new client. People may rationlize to themselves that doing an inadequate job once or twice is really "not a big deal" or "it doesn't hurt anyone in the long run." They may also stretch the truth or bad-mouth a competitor in hopes of getting a sale.

The world is a different place now. Customers may expect more than they did a few years ago. People are smarter and savvier; they expect to be treated honestly and fairly. Companies that lose sight of their essential core values will not be around for the long haul.

In the current job market, many companies are restructuring and laying off at an accelerated rate. More and more pressure is being put on various sales departments to bring in more revenue. This can create underlying fear and frustration that often results in a lack of caring, resulting in lower standards and compromising of values.

A recent survey stated that in a group of 18- to 34-year-olds, 79 percent believed that there were no absolute ethical standards. To some, this statistic may seem high, yet it may easily reflect the changes plaguing companies in the last few years. In response to increased competition, decreased market share, and lower sales, ethics have become compromised.

For example, in one company, everyone was told about the company's focus on principles and values. This topic was talked about at every level and put into practice by management. The CEO thought his job was to instill his core principles and beliefs to all levels of management. He thought that if each employee felt and lived by those values, customers would feel comfortable. They would trust the company and ultimately sales would increase. This company grew to $1 billion in annual revenue in a relatively short time.

Since then, however, a merger occurred and those core values were abandoned. Trust began to erode as employees felt the cultural shift from an emphasis on ethics to an emphasis on profit. They felt less empowered, less respected. Unfortunately, those feelings spilled over to their relationships with customers. The result was decreased sales and increased competition. This story is not unique to one company, but often heard and played out throughout many organizations.

In this time of increasing change and competition, what is the answer? The long-term solution is rooted in clearly stated values and ethics that are practiced on a daily basis. The company needs to define and communicate its vision, values, and principles. These values must be explained and clearly understood by the sales team. They need to be part of the sales presentation so that customers can understand them. Mutual trust is essential in building a foundation within a company, and it must extend to all levels and relationships in the organization. If a company communicates and practices its core values, employees will feel greater security, caring, and belief in the product. Ultimately, these feelings will be reflected in salespeople's relationships with customers.

It may seem that the pressure to make a sale drives sales professionals to violate their ethical codes or, at least, to consider doing so. But rest assured, it is only by adhering to a strong ethical belief system that you can build trusting relationships with customers, relationships that will lead to long-term sales success.

REACH AND ACHIEVE ASSOCIATES provides professional coaching and training to individuals, staff, and management of businesses of all sizes. Our goal is to create and implement strategies for developing stronger people and organizations.

ETHICAL SALESMANSHIP

A Stick in Time Saves Ten

Approximately 20 minutes
(more or less, depending on size of class)

Overview

Using any one of ten common phrases about sticks, participants will select one and relate it to the ethical position taken by their corporate leaders.

Purpose

To develop insight concerning the ethical climate by regarding it from a fresh perspective.

Group Size

Any number of individuals can participate.

Room Arrangement

If possible, arrange table groups of four participants each.

Materials

➤ Projector for transparencies or for PowerPoint slides

➤ Transparency 21.1, *"Ten 'Stick' Phrases"*

➤ Flipchart

Method

1. Introduce this activity with the proviso that what is said in the room remains in the room. Advise the group that you'd like them to protect the innocent—and perhaps the guilty—by working on an exercise that asks them to project the ethical positions of organizational leaders. However, you'd like them not to identify any one person by name.

2. Explain that one of the best ways to garner original insights is to find a connection between two unrelated things. To that

end, you'd like them to think in terms of "sticks" and to relate a "stick" phrase (such as "Stick with it") to the company's sales philosophy. That philosophy may be formally presented in a mission statement or may be informally expressed in statements made by the organizational leaders.

3. Divide the group into subgroups of four or five participants and show Transparency 21.1, *"Ten 'Stick' Phrases."* Explain that you'd like them to select any one of the phrases and relate it to some aspect of the organization's sales philosophy. (If they respond that there *is* no such philosophy, ask them to create an ideal one and then to continue with the exercise.)

   After selecting one phrase, the subgroups will explain via specific examples how the stick phrase applies to the way salespeople are expected to make sales. Or they can explain how the stick phrase may be the tone of their sales meetings. Or how a particular stick phrase relates to the training salespeople receive. Basically, participants will engage in a creative expression that combines a stick phrase with an element of their organization's sales philosophy.

4. Appoint a spokesperson from each group to meet in a breakout room or a corner of the room and to synthesize the reports from all the separate groups into one single report, in a creative fashion. They might compose a poem, a rhyme, or a rap song. They might illustrate their discussion using symbols on the flipchart. They might even make a sales "pitch" to the rest of the group, encouraging them to buy into the corporate sales philosophy.

5. Meanwhile, write the word E-T-H-I-C-S along the top of a flipchart and make columns (six in all) beneath each letter. Divide the remaining participants into six groups and challenge them to come up with as many words, related to ethical sales, as they can think of. Each word must begin with the letter ("E," "T," "H," "I," "C," or "S") assigned to them.

6. While you wait for the synthesizing spokespersons to complete their assignment, call on each team (in continued rotation, if need be) to select one word and explain its ethical significance to the rest of the class.

7. Bring closure to the exercise by having the synthesizing team make their presentation.

8. Conclude the debriefing by pointing out that the juxtaposition of initially unrelated ideas can stimulate

necessary thinking about sales and the ethical bases on which they are, ideally, made.

Variation

➤ Ask the group to come up with additional "stick" phrases, such as:

Can't beat it with a stick.
Get on the stick.
Get the short end of the stick.
Quicker than you can shake a stick at it.
Stick 'em up.
Stick around.
Stick by him.
Stick in your craw.
Stick it out.
Stick with it.
Stick out like a sore thumb.
Stick to your knitting.
Stick together.
Stick up for him.
Stick your foot in your mouth.
Stick your neck out.
Stick your nose in where it doesn't belong.

Then ask small groups to select one of the posted phrases and relate it to the ethical climate of a larger institution, for example, the presidency, Wall Street financiers, corporate America, the Olympics, the Catholic Church, the automotive industry, et cetera.

➤ Invite participants to form committees to either create or revise the organizational sales philosophy.

Discussion

➤ To what extent do the values of the organizational head cascade down to the average employee?

➤ How difficult would it be for you to challenge the tone (positive or negative) that's been established by the head of your organization?

➤ What's the connection in your organization between sales and ethics?

Quotation

"An invasion of armies can be resisted, but not an idea whose time has come."
—Victor Hugo

**Points
of Interest**

In *The Best Seller,* author D. Forbes Ley asserts, *"The problem here, as well as all across the profession of selling, is that few salespeople take the time to develop any new openings. They want to stay with what they have rather than be creative and take the chance of coming up with something new and exciting."* He suggests using the concept of mystery as a means of stimulating creative thought.

TEN
"STICK" PHRASES

1. Walk softly and carry a big stick

2. Sticks and stones may break my bones but words will never hurt me

3. Stick in the mud

4. A carrot on a stick

5. Sticky fingers

6. Stick to your guns

7. Stick it to them

8. Stickler for details

9. Stick to one's ribs

10. Stick it out

22 A Sale of Need Is a Sale Indeed

Approximately 25 minutes
(more or less, depending on size of class)

Overview

The sales process should never be one-directional, based only on the salesperson's need to sell a product or service. This exercise illustrates the importance of involving the buyer in the selling process and of ethically considering the role of need in both actual and attempted sales.

Purpose

To encourage buyer input while a sale is being conducted.

Group Size

Any number of individuals can participate. The group should be divided into subgroups of four or five.

Room Arrangement

If possible, arrange table groups for each team of four or five.

Materials

➤ An item to sell, for example, masking tape
   Optional: A bag of candy

Procedure

1. Hold up some common item—perhaps one that is in the room already, such as a roll of masking tape or a token prize that you've purchased in advance, such as a dictionary or a set of marking pens.

2. Explain that you'll allow 10 minutes for table groups to come up with a convincing sales pitch, the objective of which is to

persuade you to purchase the common item you're holding. Sales pitches should not be more than 3 minutes in length. Note that one person will serve as sales spokesperson for the group.

3. After 10 minutes, call on each spokesperson in turn and allow each up to 3 minutes to make the sales pitch. Listen carefully to learn if any one of them evinces an interest in finding out what you need.

4. After all groups have made their presentations, award the prize (or ask the class to give a standing ovation) to the table group that inquired about your needs. (If more than one group did, share the candy or have several ovations. If none did, proceed with your concluding remarks.)

5. Discuss the two-way nature of successful sales: not only should salespeople focus on what they need to sell, they should also focus on what the buyer needs to buy. The best relationships between salespeople and their customers depend on a solution-driven process, one that involves questioning, listening, and ethically aligning the customer's need with the seller's product. To make a sales only to reach a quota is simply not ethical. In time, such disregard for what customers need may lead to a loss of customers.

Variation

The concept of reciprocity (as shown in concern for the salesperson's need to sell and the buyer's need or lack of need to purchase) represents the yin/yang nature of interpersonal relationships. Thus, it can be used in any number of other training programs. Examples follow.

➤ *Listening.* Have participants work in pairs. One person speaks for a minute regarding an "easy" topic: hobby, pet, family, vacation. Before the second person can continue the conversation, he or she must paraphrase what was said by the first speaker.

➤ *Memory Development.* We often forget the names of those to whom we've been introduced because we're concerned about the impression we may be making on the person. To help participants focus on the name as it's spoken, ask the second person in a dialogue to inquire about the name before launching into his or her own introduction.

➤ *Communication.* Whether it's a letter participants have to write, a presentation they have to make, or a briefing they have to conduct, they should consider the WIIFM ("What's In It For Me?") factor: How will the recipient of the information benefit from the idea being proposed or the product being sold? Ask participants to select a forum in which they often communicate (letter, presentation, briefing) and to express their ideas with the WIIFM factor evident.

Discussion

➤ What steps can salespeople take to move from ego-centrism to other-centrism?
➤ How much do you know about your customers or clients?
➤ How much do they know about you?
➤ What do you do when you learn a client doesn't really need your product?

Quotation

"The first step in learning is confusion."
—John Dewey

Points of Interest

Lee Iacocca is regarded by many as the "salesperson of the century." And, it was Lee Iacocca himself who asserted that the best thing you could do for your career is learn to think on your feet.

ETHICAL SALESMANSHIP

Info fo' You

Approximately 45 minutes

Overview

Participants in this exercise actually write a script for an infomercial describing the product or service their organization provides. A panel of impartial judges reviews the presentations and then awards a special trophy to the winning presenters. The award is based on the ethical practice of "full disclosure."

Purpose

To encourage full disclosure regarding products or services.

Group Size

Any number of individuals can participate. The group should be divided into subgroups of four or five.

Room Arrangement

Arrange table groups for four or five participants each.

Materials

➤ Flipchart and marking pens
➤ Token prizes (perhaps books about sales or blue ribbons) for the winning team

Procedure

1. In advance, select people outside of the participant group to serve as a panel of judges. These may be people from the marketing department, already attuned to what works in persuasive selling. Or they can be potential buyers of the goods or services being sold. These judges will assess both the effectiveness of the infomercial and its ability to persuade potential buyers to make a purchase. They will also look for honesty in the presentation.

2. Ask how many have seen an "infomercial" lately. (You may wish to note that the word "infomercial" is a *portmanteau*—a new-word combination of two existing words: "information" and "commercial" in this case.) Elicit specific aspects of infomercials participants may have seen on television.

3. Ask the teams teams to select a product or service their organization offers for sale, use, or consumption. (**Note:** If participants represent several different organizations, they can select one product for the group's consideration. Or they can attempt to "sell" their city, state, or country to foreigners as a place in which to live and/or do business. In the second scenario, they can assume they represent a local or national Chamber of Commerce.)

4. First ask the groups to consider their "product" and list both the pros and cons associated with it.

5. Then ask each group to write a script for an infomercial based on the listed pros and cons. Once they've written it, they will rehearse its delivery. Tell them they will soon be presented in the infomercial format: group members sit comfortably in front of the room and exchange both information and commercial commentary with each other (as infomercial sellers actually do on television).

   Advise them that the scripts will last no more than 10 minutes each and will be delivered to a live audience—that is, the other class members. This audience, like the television audience, will not interact with the sellers.

6. As they work, have the panel come into the room and arrange for them to be seated in the back. Ensure they have paper and pencil in case they wish to take notes. Explain that they are to judge the infomercials not only on the basis of how interesting they were to watch, but also on the basis of the honesty and full disclosure made about the product or service being "sold."

7. Then ask the first group to come forward and do their infomercial. Once all groups have had the opportunity to share the infomercials they have prepared, allow the judges a few minutes to compare notes and then ask them to declare a winner. Invite them to explain the rationale behind their choice and ask how they were affected by the presentation of product pros and cons.

Variation

Ask participants to make lists of other portmanteaux that have applications to sales. Use as an example the portmanteau created by former Los Angeles Lakers' coach Pat Riley, who legally owns the word "three-peat."

Discussion

➤ How do you as a buyer respond to "truth in advertising"?

➤ In what ways is an effective salesperson like an effective trial attorney?

➤ What are both the pros and cons of full disclosure?

Quotation

"In the mountains of truth you never climb in vain."
—Friedrich Nietzsche

Points of Interest

The potential cost of dishonesty—loss of reputation and loss of customers, to say nothing of lawsuits—heavily outweighs the painful truth. There are, however, ways to be truthful without putting yourself or your product in a negative position.

In their classic book on marketing (*Positioning*, Warner Books, 1993, p. 78), authors Al Ries and Jack Trout tell the true story of a bank officer named Young J. Boozer. If this were your name, you might honestly go by the initials of Y. J. Boozer or use your middle name instead. To present reality in one of several possible expressions is not unethical. By extension, salespeople can choose what to include or exclude, as long as they are not committing "sins" of omission or commission.

Decisions to make selective factual inclusions or to present facts in a different—but still honest—fashion could have prevented the awkward occurrence that took place when a customer called the bank. He asked to speak to "Young Boozer." The switchboard operator brightly responded, "We have a lot of them around here. Which one do you want to talk to?"

24

Ethics from A to Z

Approximately 20 minutes

Overview

This exercise, which works especially well as an energizer, involves a competition of sorts. The first triad to finish listing 26 ethical sales behaviors—each starting with a different letter of the alphabet—wins a token prize.

Purpose

To broaden the salesperson's range of successful behaviors.

Group Size

Any number of individuals can participate. The group should be divided into triads.

Room Arrangement

Arrange flexible seating, so participants can easily form triads.

Materials

Optional: Three cans of alphabet soup or three boxes of alphabet cereal

Procedure

1. Announce that you are challenging the group to an informal competition, but one that will provide much "food for ethical thought."

2. Explain that each triad is to come up with 26 sentences. Each sentence must start with a letter of the alphabet, beginning with an A-verb such as "Ask. . . ." The 26th sentence will be a Z-verb such as "Zero in on. . . ." (It's also permitted to modify a verb and use the adverb as the first word of the sentence. So, they could write "Zealously guard. . . ." for their Z-verb sentence.)

3. If prizes are awarded, they will be given on the basis of the first triad to complete the assignment. That triad will share its answers. Otherwise, each group will share one portion of the 26 sentences—to avoid the information overload that would occur if each triad read all 26. For example, if there are six triads, each will take four letters of the alphabet. Triad 1 will do sentences beginning with A–D. Triad 2 will do E–H, and triad 3, I–L. Triad 4 has letters M–P. Triad 5 has Q–U and triad 6, V–Z.

Variation

The A-to-Z competition can be used with any other training program.

Discussion

➤ Aristotle's acknowledgment that we all behave (or should behave) in a foolish fashion from time to time is echoed in the words of many experts from many fields. (Einstein, for example, in working on his quantum physics theories, used to imagine himself riding a beam of light.) The element of playfulness often leads to new ideas—ideas that could be used, for example, to resolve thorny ethical issues or to generate creative ideas. What "foolish" thing can you do to increase sales—something that might make you feel foolish for a few minutes but that might pique the interest of a buyer?

➤ Which of the 26 possibilities are you not yet employing but could employ to increase sales?

➤ What other structures (not alphabetic, but perhaps numeric or alliterative) could you use to increase/ensure ethical sales behaviors? (For example, what would be the Five Steps to Making an Honest Sale? Or, what might be six P-words that would encourage ethical relationships with clients?

Quotation

"There is a foolish corner in the brain of the wisest man."
—Aristotle

Points of Interest

Harvard Professor Howard Gardner is famous for his theory of multiple intelligence and his studies of the creative personality. His research has led him to realize that creative individuals—from all walks of life—engage in three techniques: they spend time each day reflecting; they refuse to let failure shape their future actions; and they capitalize on their strengths.

In keeping with Gardner's observation, reflect on ethical behaviors in which you engaged at the end of each day. Or reflect on what you *might* have done to show greater respect, concern, and compassion for those with whom you interact each day. Discuss with a respected colleague steps you can take to prevent failures from leading you to unethical behavior. (For example, if you didn't make quota, you might be tempted to cut ethical corners in order to do so for the next month. Charting improvements with a respected colleague will help keep you on the ethical path.) List your strengths and vow that they won't ever become unethical weak spots. (To illustrate, an extremely articulate, verbal salesperson has an undeniable strength. But if he or she uses verbal adroitness unethically to persuade an unsophisticated buyer, he or she would be moving from a position of intellectual strength to one of moral weakness.)

Sell-ebrities

Approximately 45 minutes

Overview

Participants are asked to select a famous celebrity who—if money were no object—could best represent the product or service they sell. Then they are asked to identify the traits associated with that individual and to prepare a short pitch incorporating one of those traits. A subsequent discussion will reveal the importance (or apparent non-importance) of ethical qualities.

Purpose

➤ To specify the qualities associated with widely admired individuals.

➤ To plan a sales pitch that illustrates some of those qualities.

Group Size

Any number of individuals can participate. The group should be divided into subgroups of four or five.

Room Arrangement

If possible, arrange table groups for four or five participants each.

Materials

Small scraps of paper. (Each person receives a number equivalent to the number of groups minus one. If there are 20 people and four groups of five, each person would receive three sheets of paper, making 60 the total number of sheets you'll need.) **Optional:** Possible token prizes for the group with the highest sell-ability.

Method

1. Form groups of four or five and ask the group at large how many play golf. Then ask, "Are you more or less likely to buy

a product if Tiger Woods is endorsing it?" Continue the opening by asking similar questions: "How many of you admire Michael Jordan?" Then, "Do you buy Hanes underwear because he pitches it?" "How many of you enjoy Heather Locklear's acting?" Then, "Would you buy hair color because of it?" "Would Sarah Ferguson's royal status prompt you to join Weight Watchers?" And, for those with long memories, "How many of you purchased a Mr. Coffee coffee machine because Joe DiMaggio told you that you should?" (**Note:** Be sure to include both genders and realms other than the sports world.)

2. Discuss the fact that celebrities earn millions of dollars because of these endorsements. Ask how effective participants think such endorsements are.

3. Ask each group to short-list five famous people they'd like selling the product or service their organization provides, and then prioritize the list to determine their number one choice.

4. Next, have groups list the attributes they think of when they think about this person. They should select at least three specific traits or behaviors associated with this individual.

5. Ask if (and if so, how often) the word "ethical" appeared in the lists of traits. If it appeared seldom or not at all, ask the group how important ethics is in a salesperson. If it appeared frequently, simply concur in validating its importance.

6. Finally, have groups prepare a short pitch incorporating (or giving evidence of) those specific qualities. These pitches (or elements of them) are ones that salespeople can use in the future.

7. Place a pile of small pieces of paper at each table (one for each person at the table times the number of groups that will be reporting [other than their own]).

8. Ask each group to appoint one person who will come forward and deliver the pitch. Following each presentation, ask participants to score the effectiveness of the sales pitch on a scale of 1 to 10, with 10 being the highest. Collect the scraps following each group's presentation and add the numbers. Award token prizes or simply your congratulations to the winning team.

9. Let the winners bring closure to the exercise by having them discuss their selections, their final choice, the traits associated

with that person, and the way they wove those traits into their sales pitch.

10. Conclude the debriefing by pointing out that there are some qualities, like trustworthiness, that separate celebrities from "sell-ebrities." Trustworthiness is a trait a salesperson may possess even though his or her customers or prospective buyers do not know it. One way to demonstrate that customers can count on the salesperson to deal honestly is to anticipate objections and address them before the prospect can. In so doing, the salesperson can show he or she has nothing to hide. Plus, the salesperson has a chance to explain why the good points of the product or service far exceed the negative ones the prospect might bring up.

Encourage participants to be wary of name-dropping and, as consumers themselves, to discern value itself, regardless of who may be espousing it.

Variation

Ask teams of five or six to assume they've been appointed to provide a list of five possible keynote speakers for their next national sales conference. They are to assume money is no object. After 5 or 10 minutes, call on each group to share the lists. Write the names on the flipchart and then ask if anyone notices anything unusual. In all likelihood, the names will primarily be white males. (If not, congratulate the team(s) that supplied the other names.)

Point out the importance of salespeople (managers, leaders, and so forth) anticipating criticism that might arise from an honest omission and avoiding charges of sexism or racism or any other "ism" by thinking inclusively.

The exercise, with slight alteration, can also be used in diversity, leadership, and persuasion programs.

Discussion

➤ What national or international figure, living or dead, could persuade you to purchase something you really did not need?

➤ Analyze the rationale that explains why youngsters *must* have certain celebrity-endorsed products.

➤ How successful are advertisements that deliberately mismatch appeals—such as having Robert Dole and Britney Spears in the same ad? Or, the new BMW mini-movie/commercial with Marilyn Manson and James Brown?

Quotation
_____

"The two most engaging powers of an author [and possibly of a salesperson as well] are to make new things familiar and familiar things new."
—Samuel Johnson

Points of Interest
_____

Authors H. B. Karp and Bob Abramms, writing in *Training & Development* ("Doing the Right Thing," August 1992, p. 37), note two basic concerns with ethics. First, ethical behavior runs the gamut from the possession of morality and responsible behavior to behavior that is used simply to prevent someone from getting in trouble. Second, they contend, there is no one definition, no commonly agreed upon determination of what constitutes ethical behavior. They also maintain that it is ethics that converts values to action. Values, for example, set priorities while ethics set boundaries within which appropriate behavior is exercised.

ETHICAL SALESMANSHIP

News-Capers

26

Approximately 40 minutes

Overview

Participants receive newspapers and pull from them articles illustrating why the public may be losing confidence in public institutions, corporate bodies, and government agencies. Using those same reasons, participants undertake a Janusian approach to persuade buyers to purchase their product or service.

Purpose

To encourage thinking about what does and what does not constitute the organization's values.

Group Size

Any number of individuals can participate. The group should be divided into subgroups of four or five.

Room Arrangement

Arrange table groups for four or five participants each.

Materials

Copies of newspapers—they need not be from that day—so that each person has at least one section (preferably business or current events).

Method

1. Begin the exercise by asking if anyone has read about or seen a report such as the "fleecing of America" on the evening news—a report of a shoddy product or a manufacturing recall or an outright transgression of consumers' faith in a given industry or commodity or institution. If not, have a few of your own ready. (On any given day, you are likely to find headlines like the following: "Pentagon disclosures point to misconduct by top military officials in 13 states"; "$10M largest civil penalty against public company over financial

reporting"; "Agent: FAA buried lapses"; "Company guilty in Alabama pollution case."

2. Distribute newspaper sections—one for each participant. Allow at least 10 minutes for table groups to list headlines that deal with wrongdoing.

3. Next, ask the table groups to think in reverse terms: how can a negative become a positive? A story about discrimination, for example, could inspire a given organization to ensure its own practices are not discriminatory. Participants will take some of these negative ones and create opposite ones to assure their consumers that the products or services they provide have quality and value.

4. The next step asks them to think about ways to assure their clients that the misdeeds participants have read about would not be tolerated in participants' own organizations. (If the groups are composed of individuals representing several different organizations, they can select one to serve as the exemplar.) Based on one news report that showed an organization violating some ethical code, the group will explain how they converted a negative into a positive selling point for their own product or service.

5. Ask each group to make a brief presentation.

Variation

The concept of Janusian thinking dates back thousands of years to the ancient Romans, who featured the god Janus's head with two profiles on their coins. One profile looked back to the year just ended. The other looked forward to the year about to begin. (The month of January is named after Janus.) The idea of viewing a given situation from opposite perspectives can be applied to courses dealing with Critical Thinking, Problem-Solving, Strategic Planning, and Creativity.

Discussion

➤ How can an individual or organization that engaged in unethical acts recapture the public's confidence?

➤ What examples can you recall, from your own private or professional experience, of an organization that acted admirably to make amends for an egregious error?

➤ What executive-level transgression or decision would cause you to resign from your own organization?

Quotation

"There is no fire like passion, there is no shark like hatred, there is no snare like folly, there is no torrent like greed."
—Buddha

**Points
of Interest**

In its second annual listing of the "101 Dumbest Moments in Business," *Business 2.0* awards its dubious distinction first of all to Enron for assuming its aggressive accounting cover-ups would never be noticed. Also cited is overseer Arthur Andersen, whose auditors apparently failed to discover the erroneous addition of $1 billion to Enron's assets. Apart from this mega-scandal, what other nominations would you make to next year's list of dumbest business moments?

27 Inside Scoops

Approximately 30 minutes

Overview

The negative fallout from keeping customers "out of the loop" has created glaringly critical outcries from the public. Witness the recent scandals involving cars and tires that were sold despite the companies' knowledge of dangerous deficiencies or medical offices that fail to tell patients their doctors have been convicted of malpractice in other states. Participants in this exercise are asked to consider what customers want to, need to, deserve to, should, or shouldn't know about the product or service participants provide.

Purpose

To stimulate thinking about the kind of information that can or should be shared with customers without jeopardizing organizational policies.

Group Size

Any number of individuals can participate. The group should be divided into subgroups of four or five.

Room Arrangement

Arrange seating flexible enough to accommodate groups of different sizes.

Materials

➤ Handout 27.1, *"Information: Inside/Out"*

➤ Small scraps of paper, one for each participant

Method

1. Elicit examples of organizations that make their customers feel included and/or important by sharing "insider" information—delivery companies, for example, that allow the

customer access to tracking information so that they can learn the transit status of their packages.

2. Ask participants to write a number from 1 to 5 on a scrap of paper. The number indicates the degree to which their own organizations share information with customers: "1" indicates very little "insider" information is shared; "5" indicates the company is exemplary in sharing information with customers. The numbers in between represent gradations along the continuum.

3. Form groups on the basis of the numbers—all the "1"s will sit together; all the "2"s will sit together, et cetera. (The groups need not all be of the same size and probably will not be.) Have them briefly discuss why they assigned the numbers they did.

4. Distribute Handout 27.1 and allow 10 to 15 minutes for completion. (**Note:** If participants are not all from the same organization, have the subgroups select one representative organization to use in their handout matrix.)

5. Conclude the exercise by having one group sit in a "fishbowl" with the other participants seated in a circle outside the fishbowl, inner circle. Have the fishbowl group explain their handout answers while the others assume the role of customers.

6. Wrap up by having the "customers" provide feedback on the report they heard from the fishbowl group.

Variation

Consider using a real focus group to learn how customers feel or would feel about certain information-sharing changes your sales team may be considering.

1. Assemble a group of six or seven representative customers.

2. Advise them that you'd like to tape record or videotape their meeting.

3. Create a relaxed atmosphere within a structured (agenda-driven) framework and with a moderator who can refrain from becoming involved in the responses to the questions he or she poses.

4. Have the sales team in the background, taking notes on their observations but not participating in any way in the discussion.

5. The sales team should meet as soon as possible following the focus group meeting, with the original problem-solvers/decision-makers. They should evaluate their impressions and compare them to the actual tape recording. Focus group input is one valuable means of determining what customers would like to know and what they feel they need to know.

Discussion

➤ What information is "closely held" in your own organization?

➤ Does your organization have its secrets?

➤ Does the withholding of this information from your customers cross any ethical barriers?

➤ What information not now provided to customers do you feel they would appreciate having?

Quotation

"The man who is denied the opportunity of making decisions of importance begins to regard as important the decisions he is allowed to make."
—C. Northcote Parkinson

Points of Interest

In keeping with the Quality movement's definitions of "internal customers" (those who receive the output of our work) and "external customers" (those who purchase the actual product or service provided by the organization), you can extend the need-to-know idea to a Supervision class or a class dealing with Interviews or Hiring and Firing.

An important distinction supervisors need to make is that between disability and inability. According to the *Supervisor's Guide to Employment Practices,* an employee who cannot read because of dyslexia is covered under the Americans with Disabilities Act (ADA) and, in all likelihood, will have to be accommodated on the job. On the other hand, someone who cannot read because he or she never completed school may have an "inability" rather than a "disability" and therefore may not be covered.

Basically, the act states companies cannot discriminate against individuals with disabilities who are otherwise qualified to perform the basic functions of the job. Reasonable accommodations must be made to allow such individuals to do their jobs.

The difficulty in many cases, of course, is in the acquisition of the information you need. Extreme sensitivity will be required to learn what you need to know.

Information: Inside/Out

DIRECTIONS

Take 10–15 minutes to complete the questions and to fill in four quadrants regarding information and its accessibility to the public.

1. What is the primary product or service your organization provides?

2. What are the 10 most significant facts regarding that product or service?

3. How many of these does your average customer know about?

4. Complete the following matrix with reference to information about your product or service. Keep in mind these questions as you do so:

   ➤ If customers were to come in and examine our books, would they find anything that would embarrass us? Does any of the information we are not sharing constitute a legal, moral, or ethical violation?
   ➤ If I were a consumer of this product or a user of the service we provide, what do I know as an insider that I would want to know as an outsider?
   ➤ Is this information being shared with the public? Why or why not?
   ➤ Is there ever a rationale for "full disclosure"? Why or why not?
   ➤ What are the pros and cons of sharing internal information with outsiders?

Fill in the four quadrants below in relation to the product or service your organization provides. Then determine how much of that information is currently being shared.

Information that the public . . .

Would regard as nice to know	Would find necessary to know
Deserves to know	Would not regard as necessary

28

Ethics Audit

Approximately 25 minutes

Overview

This exercise affords participants an opportunity to assess their sales culture via an ethics audit. The audit follows a brief discussion of the extent to which those at the top of a sales organization or department influence the sales culture.

Purpose

To generate discussion regarding elements of the organizational culture that may need strengthening.

Group Size

Any number of individuals can participate.

Room Arrangement

No special arrangements are required.

Materials

Handout 28.1, *"Sales Culture Audit"*

Procedure

1. Point out that the recent spate of corporate scandals has roots that extend deep into the soil of immorality and illegality. Supply a few examples, such as the admission by WorldCom that it was guilty of accounting fraud—one of the largest frauds in the history of American business. They inflated profits by $3.8 billion during a 13-month period ending in March 2002. Their former CEO, Bernard Ebbers, also "borrowed" hundreds of millions of dollars from the firm.

2. Lead a brief discussion concerning the extent to which the tone of a particular culture is established by those at the top of the organization—those with sufficient clout to influence the buying and selling patterns of thousands of others.

3. Distribute Handout 28.1 and have participants work on it individually. Have small groups discuss their most extreme replies.

4. Bring closure by calling on a spokesperson from each group to share briefly the participants' replies.

Variation

Ask for a volunteer to distribute the survey organization-wide (with some word-smithing to make it applicable to any employee), after obtaining the necessary approvals, and to analyze the results. (Professional courtesy dictates the analysis be shared with senior management before it is distributed throughout the organization.)

Have participants develop their own assessment tools. They will use sentence completion continuum extremes based an analysis of existing procedures, practices, and philosophies. For example, "The quality of our produce is shoddy 1 2 3 4 5 6 7 8 9 10 best-in-class."

Have them discuss where ethical lines are being crossed, thus creating potentially serious consequences for the individual (and his or her job), the team, the department, and even the organization. Have participants compare their assessments and—if several participants work in the same department—create a synthesized tool that can be taken back to the workplace and used to create and enforce ethical policies.

Discussion

What drives people to remain silent despite their knowledge of wrongdoing?

What is or should be your organization's procedure for whistleblowers to follow?

What ethical tone is being set in your own organization by those in authority?

Quotation

"If we could read the secret history of our enemies, we should find in each man's life, sorrow and suffering enough to disarm all hostility."
—Henry Wadsworth Longfellow

**Points
of Interest**

Speaking of the need to rid the whole culture of unethical practices and not just isolate a small number of people or practices, management consultant Frank J. Navran uses the metaphor of a "flea dip." He likens the elimination of a particular ethical problem to a flea dip—which will remove fleas from your pet . . . until it returns to its everyday environment. There, in all likelihood, the animal will pick up fleas once again.

Navran maintains the establishment of an ethical environment depends on two things:

➤ Putting the right people in the right place.

➤ Rewarding the people who are behind the change efforts.

Sales Culture Audit

DIRECTIONS

Circle the number that comes closest to the description you feel best applies to your organization.

Sales Environment

1. Relationship between sales manager and staff is:

| Demeaning, impersonal | 1 2 3 4 5 6 7 8 9 10 | Encouraging, supportive |

2. Top decision-makers:

| Are profit-driven above all else | 1 2 3 4 5 6 7 8 9 10 | Place equal weight on profit and values |

3. Organizational leaders:

| Reflect poorly on the firm's integrity | 1 2 3 4 5 6 7 8 9 10 | Make us proud to be working in this firm |

4. Advertising for our products is:

| Negative, focused on sex or violence | 1 2 3 4 5 6 7 8 9 10 | Fun, wholesome, honest |

5. Relationships among sales staff can be described as:

| Dog-eat-dog, secretive, highly competitive | 1 2 3 4 5 6 7 8 9 10 | Sharing, cooperative, harmonious |

Ethical Environment

6. Customers:

| Are misled, taken advantage of | 1 2 3 4 5 6 7 8 9 10 | Are given a fair deal |

7. Vendors are viewed as:

| A source of irritation | 1 2 3 4 5 6 7 8 9 10 | Partners in the manufacturing/ sales process |

8. The product or service we provide is:

| Not one I'd recommend to my family | 1 2 3 4 5 6 7 8 9 10 | Among the best you can find anywhere |

9. Competitors are:

| Badmouthed, mocked to customers | 1 2 3 4 5 6 7 8 9 10 | Referred to and treated respectfully |

10. In sales meetings:

| Agendas are hidden | 1 2 3 4 5 6 7 8 9 10 | Issues are dealt with honestly and openly |

INTERPRETATION

If your score is less than 50, there's a good possibility your organization is consumed by the profit factor. While this is not necessarily a bad thing, if the drive toward profit reaches greed levels, it can dominate the decisions being made and actions being taken. It's also possible that your score reflects dissatisfaction with either the company you've chosen to work for or your chosen profession itself. To ascertain further if the dissatisfaction your score reflects is widely held, make a copy of the culture assessment and ask at least five colleagues to fill it out. Compare your answers with theirs.

If you scored from 50 to 70, your organization could probably be regarded as average in terms of the value it places on values themselves. There's room for improvement here. Consider ways to effect that improvement.

A score of 71 to 89 reflects a company that probably won't make the list of Top 100 Companies to Work for in America. Nonetheless, all the right ingredients are here for a culture of ethical success. Refinement is called for in some areas but, in all likelihood, there are no glaring gaps between what's right and what's being done.

Your firm, if you rated it 90 or above, might easily qualify for that Top 100 list. It would appear you are proud of your association with this organization and with the product or service it offers customers. As good as the organization is, though, a commitment to continuous improvement will keep it good and perhaps make it outstanding. Remember the Lexus ad: "The relentless pursuit of perfection."

ETHICAL SALESMANSHIP

Take the "Ow" Out of "Now"

Approximately 20 minutes

Overview

"Now" is one of the words to which potential buyers are most likely to respond. Participants in this exercise are tasked with identifying key words that attract customers. They are also shown a list of persuasive words. Then, they are given a product for which to prepare an advertisement that uses some of these words in an ethical fashion and one that uses them unethically.

Purpose

To provide participants with a list of words that can be used to describe a product or service—ideally, in an ethical fashion.

Group Size

Any number of individuals can participate. The group should be divided into an even number of subgroups.

Room Arrangement

Arrange two, four, or six table groups of three to six participants each.

Materials

➤ Flipchart and marking pens
➤ Projector for transparencies or for PowerPoint slides
➤ Transparency 29.1, *"Words That Work"*
➤ Handout 29.1, Article: *"Your" Key to Closing More Sales*

Procedure

1. Begin with a discussion of "trigger words," both positive and negative, that influence participants as buyers. A positive

trigger word might be "free," for example. Negative trigger words might be "limited number" because consumers may feel these words are simply a ploy, trying to manipulate them into buying something immediately. (If time permits, extend the discussion to positive and negative trigger words that affect them as employees.)

2. Write these words on a flipchart sheet that has two columns: one for the positive words and one for the negative.

3. Next, discuss the ethics of using certain words and phrases. Note the political campaigns employing negative ads. Cite examples of words that appeal to our fears or that seem to capitalize on tragedy. You might even discuss situations in which the right words were used at the wrong time, such as the eulogies for Senator Paul Wellstone that seemed more like campaign rallies in the eyes of many. Comment on the fact that words are neutral terms—different people react to them in different ways. Words that typically have a positive impact on buyers could, when used inappropriately, have just the reverse effect. And words that some people regard as negative could even, in some situations, have a positive effect. An example might be the popularity of books for "dummies" and for "idiots."

4. Then note the positive words that have typically proven successful in swaying consumers to actually make a purchase. One of them is the word "now." Used with the best intentions—for example, concern for customer's needs—it is most appropriate to encourage immediate action. But, if a false sense of urgency is created, if consumers are manipulated into making a decision before they've had sufficient time to consider it, "ow" consequences could result. The customer may feel pressured to buy, for example, and may come back the next day to return the product. If the seller lied about imminent danger, of course, such statements would be unethical. Exaggerating, for example, the likelihood of a chemical warfare attack in order to sell gas masks would be wrong.

5. Show Transparency 29.1, *"Words That Work,"* which contains persuasive words. Divide the group into an even number of subgroups. (Each subgroup, ideally, will have the same number of participants.)

6. Explain that half the subgroups will be asked to develop an ad (using at least three words on the list or on the flipchart) that makes an ethical appeal to potential buyers. The other half of

the subgroups will create an ad using at least three words from the transparency list or the flipchart list. Their ad will make an unethical or manipulative appeal to potential buyers.

7. Once they understand the instructions, give them the actual physical object they will be writing an ad for. Take some item in the room or on your person (a wallet, a watch, a pen) and place it in a prominent position. Tell participants to write their ads to sell that object. Groups will have about 15 minutes to do this.

Variation

Invite, if possible, the head of the sales department to select the ad he or she feels is most persuasive. Discuss the use, misuse, and abuse of words from an ethical perspective, using that person's selection as a starting point.

Distribute Handout 29.1, the article on guerrilla selling, *"'Your' Key to Closing More Sales,"* by Don Cooper, and discuss the points made.

Discussion

➤ How sophisticated do you feel the average consumer is?

➤ What prompts you to make the purchases you make?

➤ What phrases turn you off? Why?

Quotation

"The simple act of paying attention can take you a long way."
—Keanu Reeves

Points of Interest

John R. Graham, president of Graham Communications in Quincy, Massachusetts, heads a marketing services and sales consulting firm. He advises clients to eliminate negative statements or those that may create an impression that is negative. For example, saying, "They didn't get back to me" suggests you are not willing to take the initiative to find out what you or a client needs to know. Consider the negative implications associated with the following phrases:

➤ "I thought someone else was taking care of that."

➤ "I didn't know you wanted me to do that."

➤ "I didn't think about that."

➤ "As I understand it . . . "

➤ "I've been trying to get everyone together, but . . ."

WORDS THAT WORK

Discover
Save
Easy
Guarantee
Love
Money
New
Proven
Results
You

Article: *"Your" Key to Closing More Sales*

DON COOPER

One of the most powerful words in a salesperson's verbal arsenal is "your." While most salespeople focus on "our products," "our services," and "the history of our company," top sales performers prefer to talk about "your needs," "your experiences," and "your results."

As a customer, you don't think about the salesperson, their product, or their commission. You think about how the product or service might solve your problem. You think about your budget and your priorities. You think about how the product makes you feel. Savvy salespeople tap into those thoughts and emotions by using the word "your" liberally in their questioning and in their presentation.

Here's how one sales pro, Dana Stephenson of San Diego Harley-Davidson, uses this tactic to sell more to her customers: "As soon as a person tries on a piece of clothing, I start referring to it as 'yours.' I say things like, 'Let me see how your shirt looks.' 'Would you like me to hold your jacket while you try on these other items?' and 'Do you have the shoes to complete your outfit?'"

As Dana noted, "When you refer to something as 'your' item, in the customer's mind, they already own it. So they stop thinking about whether or not they want to buy it. The sale is already closed."

Reprinted with permission from Don Cooper, 2802 Sundown Lane, #203, Boulder, Colorado 80303.

DON COOPER—"America's Networking Guru"—is a sales and marketing expert who speaks, writes, and consults on how to attract and keep more customers. He is a contributing author of *Confessions of Shameless Self Promoters* with Debbie Allen and Jay Conrad Levinson. You can contact Don by phone at 303-449-1389 or 303-885-1182 or by e-mail at Don@DonCooper.com. You can also find other articles at www.DonCooper.com.

30 Fine Lines vs. Fine Lines

Approximately 30 minutes

Overview

This activity invites debate regarding two kinds of lines: lines salespeople may be using—lines that are perfectly fine—and lines that may be crossed when those fine lines have an ulterior, and perhaps unethical, motive. Participants work on strategies for overcoming objections and then discuss if and when the objection-overcoming strategies are used inappropriately.

Purpose

➤ To acquire useable lines for overcoming objections.

➤ To consider when these lines constitute a crossing of ethical boundary lines.

Group Size

Any number of individuals can participate. The group should be divided into subgroups of four or five.

Room Arrngement

Any setting that accommodates small-group clusters will work.

Materials

➤ Handout 30.1, *"Does It Cross the Line?"*

➤ Flipchart

Procedure

1. Solicit participants' experiences regarding customers' objections. Have them share both their successful lines, used to overcome objections, and their analyses of why their best efforts failed to make the sale.

2. Next, form subgroups of four or five. Ask participants to list five of the most common objections they hear.

3. After 5 minutes, begin to compile a list on the flipchart by calling on a spokesperson from each group to give the objections. Eliminate duplicates from the list.

4. If these common objections are not provided by the spokespersons, add them to the list: "The budget won't allow it." "I can get it somewhere else for less." "I'm satisfied with my current vendor (or with the current product)."

   Have participants, still working in small groups, take about 10 minutes to write down lines they feel would work best to overcome the objections listed on the flipchart. When they've finished, call on a spokesperson from each group to share one line that works to overcome objections.

5. Distribute Handout 30.1, "Does It Cross the Line?", and have the groups respond to the questions.

6. Conclude with a discussion of answers provided to the handout questions.

Variation

Have participants consider their "spheres of influence" when trying to overcome objections. Typically, the phrase refers to the range to which one's influence extends. So in the conventional sense of the term, various individuals in various communities might be willing to listen to a salesperson's ideas and to be influenced by them.

Have participants graphically depict a sphere of influence with concentric circles representing the numerous areas in which they might find influence tools for overcoming objections. For example, in the innermost circle would be the salesperson and the prospect. (The salesperson would use some of the lines discussed in this exercise.)

The next circle, surrounding this core one, might be former customers, who could be called upon to provide testimonials that might help persuade a reluctant buyer. Another, larger circle might be accrediting institutions of one sort or another. For example, if a particular hotel had won the President Award for Exemplary Service for the last 3 years, that fact could be used to convince a prospect that he or she would be treated well when making plans for a conference at that location.

Expand the number of circles and their respective tools as you gain experience.

Discussion

➤ Have you ever felt uncomfortable after you've successfully turned a prospect into a buyer?

➤ How do you think the negative connotations surround the phrase "used car salesperson" originated?

➤ Could any of these connotations be applied to the way your company pitches sales?

Quotation

"The Willy Lomans aren't making it today."
—Bernard Rosenbaum

Points of Interest

Cliff Ennico is the host of the PBS television series "MoneyHunt." He is also an author who takes an occasional contrarian view. In "Cynical? Insecure? Ruthless? You're Hired! Essential Characteristics for Sales Success" (*Sales and Marketing* [SAM] magazine, May/June 2001, p. 62), he explores the kind of line-crossing explored in this exercise. He encourages salespeople to look hard at the reasons why people buy and to stop deluding themselves with pretty pictures. Being cynical, he maintains, means looking at both surface and subterranean reasons why people make purchases. Insecurity, he asserts, can actually help drive a salesperson to more sales. Finally, being ruthless means not letting anything (except legal and ethical issues) get in your way.

Does It Cross the Line?

CASE STUDY

There is sometimes a fine line between using an objection-overcoming line for mutually profitable purposes and using it for self-aggrandizing purposes. John Smith, a sales representative for a computerized point-of-sale system, considers only the number of sales he makes each month and not the rationale behind those sales.

John has been in the business long enough to understand how flattery works, especially to overcome the most common attitude he encounters. That attitude is the "show-me" one, voiced in the form of an objection that asks, "Why should I buy from you?"

So, as part of his sales pitch, he asks prospects if they are "serious" buyers. He goes on to say that that business owners who are truly serious about saving money rank "5" on a scale that places most business people well below that number. Before delivering his pitch, he asks them a series of questions, designed to elicit self-descriptions that place them well above average in terms of their money-saving tendencies.

Once prospects have been jointly labeled "serious" (by both John and the prospect), John then proceeds to tell prospects how his system will save them money, even if they are satisfied with their current system, even if his system costs more than competing systems they may be considering.

"It works like a charm," he boasts. "It's never failed me yet. I get people to buy whether or not they really need our point-of-sale system. Of course, it's a quality system and it really will save them money," he is fond of saying.

QUESTIONS

1. If you "win" a sale, it suggests that someone else "loses"—viz., the customer. What can you do to ensure your sales are win/win encounters?
2. If a prospect tells you his or her current system is working fine, would you ever consider agreeing with the prospect and choosing not to sell anything at that point?
3. On what occasions have you (or other salespeople you know) crossed the ethical line by using a winning line on an unsophisticated buyer?

Ethical
Management

INTRODUCTION
The Manager's Responsibility for the Ethical Office

NAN DEMARS

Robert MacGregor, former president of the Minnesota Center for Corporate Responsibility, once told me he has the same discussion with every assistant he has ever hired. On the first day of the job, he tells them: *"I'm going to be going 100 miles per hour. You will be going 120 miles per hour to stay ahead of me. In my haste to get a job done by deadline, if I ever appear to be cutting corners or sliding into unethical practices in any regard, I WANT you to stop me. It is YOUR responsibility to keep me on the ethical track. In other words, I want you to be my ethical monitor."*

That's my dream! If every manager would have that conversation with every employee he or she supervises, we would be well underway to establishing and maintaining the Ethical Office.

The Ethical Office is a *culture that fosters mutual respect, trust, and honest communication among co-workers, customers, and vendors.* The concept is becoming another means for achieving competitive advantage, as companies increasingly see the link between healthy profits and ethical cultures.

As a result, organizations today are:

➤ Writing extensive codes of ethics and conduct.

➤ Expanding employee handbooks for guidelines.

➤ Incorporating ethics training (with discussions of reality-based case studies).

➤ Creating ethics hotlines (often anonymous).

➤ Hiring ethics directors.

➤ Establishing ethics departments or appointing a human resource representative "point person" whom employees can approach with ethical dilemmas.

This aggressive approach to championing the Ethical Workplace is paying off in the following high dividends:

➤ *Productivity*—Ethical employees outperform all others. They sell more products, receive fewer calls requesting service on products sold, and post superior profit margins. The "personality" of an ethical office is healthy, energized, forward-looking, confident, creative, and resourceful. It's a real "can-do" place to work because people are not confused about what is expected of them; nor are they stressed to distraction.

➤ *Accountability*—With a clear understanding of what is expected of them, employees take responsibility and feel accountable for their personal behavior and performance, regardless of their position. They take responsibility to resolve ethical dilemmas. They place high value on personal integrity.

➤ *Communication*—Employees *want* to talk about ethical dilemmas as they arise. The manager who encourages this open communication will enjoy earlier resolution of problems and less confusion (two cost-saving advantages).

➤ *Confidentiality*—Information is power, and the unethical office shares power and information with anyone and everyone. Managers should emphasize the importance of treating as confidential information that is shared in private, information that pertains to performance reviews, information that may be based on rumor, et cetera. Everyone wins when confidences and privacy issues are respected.

➤ *Stability*—Employees *stay* in an ethical atmosphere, and that is cost saving in itself. The unethical office results in a revolving door in the human resources department. Further, the costs associated with the departure of disgruntled employees along with the resulting hiring of new employees are always high.

➤ *Predictability*—The Ethical Office is not blindsided by surprises such as harassment lawsuits and compromised security. In an ethical culture, employees address ethical dilemmas as they surface and nip them in the bud before they get out of hand.

Employees *want* to do the right thing—and they also want to trust the people they work with every day. It is the manager's responsibility to create the safe atmosphere of an Ethical Workplace for their employees. The rewards will be overwhelming.

NAN DEMARS is an office ethics trainer/consultant and author of *You Want Me To Do* What? (Simon & Schuster). She conducts training throughout the United States and in foreign countries. In addition, she is president of Executary Services, a seminar/search/office ethics consultant firm in Minneapolis.

ETHICAL MANAGEMENT

Ethics Evaluation

31

Mike Morrell

Approximately 60 minutes
(longer if there are more than three subgroups)

Overview

Many companies have written policies on ethics that are distributed on paper or are available on an intranet. In this exercise, leaders and managers are able to sharpen their awareness and understanding of the policy by "playing" with it in a learning situation.

Purpose

To enable participants to learn what the official ethics policy means to them and how they and colleagues would contribute to enforcing that policy.

Group Size

Any number of individuals can participate. The group should be divided into subgroups of four or five.

Room Arrangement

Arrange flexible seating to permit table groups of four or five.

Materials

➤ Handout 31.1, *"Directions"*

➤ Flipchart and marking pens

➤ Copies of the ethics policy being considered. (**Note:** If participants represent several different organizations, select one representative policy and make copies of it.)

Procedure

1. Lead a brief discussion of the importance of having an official ethics policy and having it well publicized in the organization.

Include mention of the fact that guidelines are useful for the unclear "gray" areas of proper, ethical behavior as well as the more obvious "black-and-white" areas. Note, too, that when policy has been breached, the organization has the legal protection of having made policy clear. Violators, in other words, knew what they were doing.

Elicit input from participants regarding their knowledge of their organization's policy and the extent of its dissemination.

2. Distribute written copies of the ethics policy to be used in the exercise and allow sufficient time for people to read it.

3. Give each participant a copy of Worksheet 31.1, *"Directions."* Allow at least 30 minutes for completion.

4. Form subgroups to share their worksheet insights.

5. Have a spokesperson from each subgroup in turn present the subgroup's findings for a plenary session.

6. Highlight the differences in the way the policy is interpreted by the various subgroups and in the way it is applied.

7. Lead a discussion on whether these differences are acceptable.

8. Ask for suggestions to improve the clarity of the policy and the guidelines for applying it.

9. Ask for volunteers who are willing to pass on these suggestions to the policymakers. Commend them for being self-confident enough to speak to senior management about possible changes in the ethics policy.

10. Wrap up by discussing ways the ethics policy can be more fully applied.

Variation

Have subgroups prepare an ideal ethics policy. Have them exchange and critique each other's policy.

Take a macrocosmic perspective: Ask subgroups to prepare an ethics policy for the industry as a whole or for political, educational, religious leaders, et cetera.

Discussion

➤ What forces may have influenced the originators of the organizational policy being studied?

➤ How often should such a policy be revisited/revised?

➤ Should the policy reflect input from every organizational level?

➤ If so, how could that input be obtained and incorporated?

➤ Should the policy reflect input from those outside the organization?

➤ If so, what particular groups should be invited to contribute their thoughts?

Quotation

"Everyone is a genius at least once a year."
—Georg Christoph Lichtenberg

Points of Interest

Authors Michael Beer and Russell Eisenstat have identified six "silent killers" related to strategy implementation. Too many managers, they maintain, avoid confronting these killers. Relate these killers to the successful implementation of an ethics policy; take into consideration what has been or could be circumvented in your own organization's efforts to create an ethical culture via issuing a policy.

➤ Top-down or laissez-faire senior management style.

➤ Unclear strategy and conflicting priorities.

➤ Ineffective senior management team.

➤ Poor vertical communication.

➤ Poor coordination across functions, businesses, or borders.

➤ Inadequate down-the-line leadership skills and development.

MIKE enjoys the process of discovering what it means to be a human being. He sees organizations and organizational development as the product of—and the current environment for—the further development of and interplay between individuals. He facilitates both organizational and individual staff development in the roles of trainer, coach, consultant, and change manager.

Directions

DIRECTIONS

1. Review the written policy and identify the parts that are clear to you and the parts that are less clear.

2. Describe what you believe this policy requires of you.

3. Describe how you (or others) ensure that the policy is understood by employees.

4. Give one or two examples of situations in your day-to-day work in which this policy is especially applicable or relevant.

5. For each example, describe how you or others monitor whether the policy is being applied.

6. For each example, describe what your actions would be if you found out the policy was being violated.

7. Note the differences among the members of your group with regard to points 1 through 6.

8. Present your results at the plenary session.

ETHICAL MANAGEMENT

Rites, Rights, and Wrongs

Approximately 30 minutes

Overview

The focus of this exercise is the delicate balance between one's right to act as he or she wishes and the effects those individual actions can have on others. Participants are asked to prepare a script that has one employee suggesting to another that while he or she enjoys the right of free speech, free expression sometimes needs to be tempered in order to avoid offending others.

Purpose

➤ To explore the issue of the individual's right to express controversial, religious, or political views in the workplace

➤ To encourage appropriate expression of those views

Group Size

Any number of individuals can participate in this exercise.

Room Arrangement

Arrange seating flexible enough to accommodate a fishbowl arrangement with one small group (of five or six participants) on the inside and a ring of observers circling them. (**Note:** If the class size is greater than 15, have two fishbowls concurrently.)

Materials

➤ Handout 32.1, "Chestnuts Roasting"

Method

1. Begin with a discussion of "rites" and "rights." Use as an example college initiation rites, some of which encourage excessive drinking. While a 21-year-old has the right to drink as much as he chooses, a moral question arises: Is it right for his fraternity brothers to encourage excesses that could be

injurious, if not fatal? Think of other rites that resulted in infringements of rights, such as the behaviors that led to the Tailhook scandal. Actions that one may have the right to engage in may lead to ethical pitfalls if they impinge on the rights of others to be treated respectfully and safely.

2. Distribute Handout 32.1, *"Chestnuts Roasting,"* and have triads work on it for 15 to 20 minutes.

3. Ask one triad to sit in the center of the room while the other participants sit on the outside of the "fishbowl" and take notes as they watch the script enacted.

4. Have the outsiders refer to their notes and share their input regarding what worked well to encourage Vincent to change his behavior or be more cautious in his remarks.

5. Debrief by asking for input from the entire group on ways to respect one person's rights without infringing on the right of all persons in a workplace to be treated respectfully. Conclude with a reference to current events if possible and with the reminder that verbal calibrations are part of the continuous-improvement path toward ethics in the workplace.

Variation

➤ Ask each triad for the one line from the script they felt would be most effective in circumstances such as these. Record the lines on a flipchart and encourage participants to make note of them and to use them in the future.

➤ Although the telling of "war stories" can be a waste of instructional time, if the contributions are guided, many valuable lessons can be learned. Have triads discuss some of the worst things that have ever been said to them by a manager—statements that may have been unethical, illegal, or perhaps simply hurtful. Have them vote on the worst horror story and ask each triad to tell that story in less than 3 minutes. (Warn them in advance that you may have to interrupt to get to the point.)

Discussion

➤ What examples can you cite of a rite or right that, if carried to an extreme, can become a wrong?

➤ What civil rights do you feel are being or have been abrogated in America today?

➤ If you were to champion a cause, what would it be?

➤ Are there rights that others opposed to your cause would say you are violating?

Quotation

"In the world that is coming, if you can't navigate differences, you've had it."
—Robert Hughes

Points of Interest

As reported in the *Democrat and Chronicle*, mega-mogul Ted Turner addressed students at Harvard Law School in April 2001. His topic: *"Our Common Future."* His remarks included these:

➤ "But, you know, communism is an endangered species."

➤ "When I offend people, I apologize. I've apologized to just about every group around. I'll even apologize to you."

as well as an explanation of these earlier remarks:

➤ "Christianity is a religion for losers."

➤ "The pope is an idiot."

➤ "The U.S. has some of the dumbest people in the world."

➤ "Fidel Castro is a hell of a guy."

➤ "The First Commandment is obsolete."

Discuss the ethics of making remarks that we are all entitled to make. Then, lead to the "cognitive dissonance" that results when a person we are prepared to dislike shows a different, and very likeable side of his or her persona:

➤ As the nation's largest single landowner, Ted Turner has pledged that his 1.7 million acres will be preserved in their natural state in perpetuity.

➤ The Turner Foundation gives $50 million annually for environmental activities.

➤ In 1997, he contributed $1 billion to programs connected with the United Nations.

➤ He has donated $250 million to his newly formed Nuclear Threat Initiative, dedicated to safely disposing of nuclear waste material and stopping the spread of nuclear and biological weapons.

Conclude by pointing out that the ethical realm is a difficult one to define. It reflects the confusion and contradictions of the "age of paradox" in which we live. Before we make judgments about individuals, we must obtain all the facts. Even when we have all the facts, it doesn't necessarily mean the individual was correct in the things he or she said. The best workplaces permit and even encourage ongoing dialogs about offenses that may be innocently given but definitely taken.

Chestnuts Roasting

CASE STUDY

Vincent Arturo is an immensely likeable fellow. There is no pretense about him. He tends to say what's on his mind—without artifice and, sometimes, without forethought. Because he founded and continues to sponsor a mentoring program in the organization, he's been asked to address the "Ceiling Smashers," a women's group within the organization, dedicated to the advancement of women and minorities.

You attended the conference and cringed when he made these remarks:

> *"I want to acknowledge my secretary, Sue. She's that pretty little thing sitting in the front row. And yes, she's had to pull my chestnuts out of the fire on more than one occasion."*

> *"Spaghetti-spinners like me know the importance of family support."*

> *"I see none of you are barefoot and only two of you are pregnant. Good. That means you're making progress."*

As Vincent's manager, you've decided to speak with him regarding his remarks. While you're certain he meant no one any harm, you're equally certain others took offense—having seen and heard the reactions of the audience.

Prepare a script with your group, showing what you would say as a manager and what Vincent's likely response would be. (Remember, the purpose behind every managerial chat of this nature is to effect improvement.) You may be called upon to enact the script in a fishbowl setting.

ETHICAL MANAGEMENT

33 That Feather in Your Cap

Regina Robertson

Approximately 35 minutes

Overview

The case study in this exercise helps participants explore the ethical issues associated with credit earned and credit due. When credit is stolen, trust begins to erode. This exercise deals with handling the stolen-credit situation in order to restore an ethical balance.

Purpose

➤ To encourage thought and discussion regarding trust-destroying instances that may require employees to challenge a manager's action.

➤ To develop positive approaches for handling situations when such a challenge is necessary.

Group Size

Any number of individuals can participate. The group should be divided into subgroups of four or five.

Room Arrangement

If possible, arrange table groups for four or five participants each.

Materials

Handout 33.1, *"Case Study"*

Procedure

1. Ask participants how they would interpret this statement, one that a government employee says he would like to deliver to his supervisor one day: "That feather in your cap came out of my tail!"

2. Discuss possible reasons to explain why some supervisors take credit that isn't rightfully theirs and why others are more inclined to acknowledge their employees' contributions.

3. Distribute Handout 33.1, *Case Study,* and ask table groups to discuss the real-world scenario and discuss the related questions.

4. On conclusion of the discussion, begin a flipchart list of "10 Commanagements"—"commandments" that supervisors/managers would ideally follow to create the best of all management worlds. Call on one spokesperson from each group to contribute one recommendation, stated as a "shall" or "shall not" sentence related to valuing employees' contributions.

Variation

Compile several lists of "Commanagements" related to various issues that arise during the course of a training session. Participants will often contribute to discussions their thoughts related to management or inequities or the culture. Encourage participants to compile these lists with co-workers upon their return to the workplace or to add to those already started in the classroom. Then encourage novel approaches (in the form of "commanagements") to some of the problems and issues identified.

Discussion

➤ What prompts some supervisors to steal credit from others?

➤ The Quality guru, Dr. W. Edwards Deming, believed the workplace should be a source of cooperation and harmony, so that workers would feel comfortable sharing their ideas about improvement. When hostility and autocratic behavior dominate the workplace, he believed, employees are reluctant to participate fully in the improvement process. How can you relate Dr. W. Edwards Deming's insistence on "driving out fear" to events in the workplace?

➤ Jack Welch, former CEO of General Electric, often speaks about confidence. Explore the effects—both positive and negative—of confidence and a lack of confidence.

Quotation

"Few things can help an individual more than to place responsibility on him, and to let him know that you trust him."
–Booker T. Washington

**Points
of Interest**

In *The Power of Positive Thinking in Business* (The Free Press, 2001) author Scott W. Ventrella lists these characteristics associated with positive thinkers:

➤ Optimism

➤ Enthusiasm

➤ Belief

➤ Integrity

➤ Courage

➤ Confidence

➤ Determination

➤ Patience

➤ Calmness

➤ Focus

Correlate these to the case study presented.

REGINA ROBERTSON is a management and leadership director. She has been employed by the federal government for 24 years. She also owns and operates her own business and training media company, Bells and Whistles.

Case Study

SITUATION

John Foster is an employee in the finance department of XYZ company. His immediate supervisor is Dave Albright. A firm believer in continuous improvement, John has noticed certain changes that could be made to improve the company—changes that would require top-level approval to implement. One day, John decides to take the initiative and write up an improvement report to submit to the CEO of XYZ. Before submitting the report, though, John asks Dave to review it. Days later, John learns his report has been submitted to the CEO. The problem? Dave has put *his* name on the report instead of John's. To compound the difficulty of the situation, John hears the CEO is preparing to give a cash award for the report . . . to *Dave.*

DISCUSSION

➤ Discuss similar situations that have happened to you or someone you know.

➤ Describe in detail three approaches that will resolve this situation without causing harm to John's career.

➤ Describe in detail three ways in which the situation could have been avoided.

➤ Describe changes or repercussions that could result from this situation.

34 Alphabet Soup-ervision

Approximately 25 minutes
(more or less, depending on size of class)

Overview

Everyday acronyms are given new meaning in this exercise and then are related to ethical situations that managers may need to resolve.

Purpose

To encourage creative thinking regarding ethical decisions managers may face.

Group Size

Any number of individuals can participate. The group should be divided into subgroups of three or four.

Room Arrangement

If possible, arrange table groups for three or four participants each.

Materials

➤ Handout 34.1, *"Acronymically Yours"*

➤ **Optional:** Bag of candy

Procedure

1. Introduce the exercise by citing Michael Michalko, author of *Thinkertoys,* a book designed to improve thought processes. Michalko believes that geniuses force relationships among things; they create new structures, new patterns of thought. Tell participants that today, you're going to ask them to force some relationships that will, ideally, lead to new approaches to old management problems.

2. Form the class into small groups of three or four participants each.

3. Distribute Handout 34.1, *Acronymically Yours,* and permit at least 15 minutes for its completion.

4. Bring closure to the exercise by asking a spokesperson from each group to report on the work the group has done, noting

especially a new solution for a management problem encased in the new acronym meaning.

Variation

The practice of forcing relationships between things not usually connected will benefit those seeking to improve their verbal fluidity or ability to think on their feet. Provide any series of letters, such as F-I-K-D-E, and challenge teams to create as many full sentences as they can within 5 minutes. The only rules are that the sentences must contain a subject and a predicate, must relate to the topic of ethics, and must not use any given word more than once. An example of this combination would be "Favorite Inspectors Kindle Desirable Ethics"—not a literary masterpiece, but a sentence nonetheless.

Discussion

➤ What are some unethical issues surrounding innovative thought—for example, the violations of copyright laws?

➤ What steps has your organization taken to ensure intellectual property is protected?

➤ What could your organization do to promote genius-thinking without making employees feel their ideas are being "ripped off"?

Quotation

"The fool wonders, the wise man asks."
–Benjamin Disraeli

Points of Interest

These are the other seven strategies[1] Michalko offers for those who want to think like a genius:

➤ Looking at problems in many different ways.

➤ Making thoughts visible.

➤ Demonstrating immense productivity.

➤ Making novel combinations.

➤ Thinking in opposite terms.

➤ Thinking metaphorically.

➤ Preparing for chance.

Ask participants to relate these to ethical dilemmas they have faced in the past.

[1] Reprinted with permission from "Thinking Like a Genius," by Michael Michalko, *Window on the Future,* http:/www.newhorizons.org.

Acronymically Yours

DIRECTIONS

Step 1: These are common acronyms in the world of business. For each, replace the actual meaning with a group-created, work-related meaning. For example, instead of "Request for Quotation," RFQ could be replaced with "Reasons for Quitting."

Acronym	Current Meaning	New Meaning
WIIFM	What's In It For Me?	_____
NIMBY	Not In My Backyard	_____
FYI	For Your Information	_____
ASAP	As Soon As Possible	_____
PDQ	Pretty Darn Quick	_____
CC	Carbon Copy	_____
KISS	Keep It Simple, Silly	_____
BTW	By The Way	_____
GMTA	Great Minds Think Alike	_____

Step 2: Select any one of the new meanings and, as a group, discuss it in relation to these prompts.

1. Considering the new meaning, what direct, ethics-related experience have you (or others you know or know of) had with it? (For example, have you ever felt like quitting [RFQ] because of an unethical action taken by your manager? What prevented you from quitting? Or, do you regret quitting?)

2. How was the situation resolved or does it continue to this day?

3. If you could create the perfect circumstances surrounding this issue, what would you do that is not already being done?

ETHICAL MANAGEMENT

Manager— Management

Approximately 30 minutes

Overview

Nonmanipulative communication is the focal point of this exercise, which asks participants to consider the ethics of strategies involved in both upward and downward communicating. The reporting stage of the exercise fosters good listening and quick thinking.

Purpose

➤ To examine the communication process.
➤ To explore the ethical aspects of steps in that process.

Group Size

Any number of individuals can participate. Participants will first work alone and then in pairs.

Room Arrangement

No special arrangements are required.

Materials

➤ Projector for transparencies or for PowerPoint slides
➤ Transparency 35.1, *"Upward Communication"*

Procedure

1. Begin with a brief discussion of the three types of communication in the business world: "upward," to those in positions higher than one's own; "downward," to those serving in subordinate positions; and "lateral," to those on the same organizational level. Ask how the tone of such communications will differ.

2. Ask participants to work in pairs. (**Note:** If there is one person "left over," he or she can form a triad with some pair and can serve as an observer.) Ask them to assume that one person in the partnership is the employee and the other person is his or her manager.

3. Ask the "subordinate" to work alone at first by listing at least five key points in communicating upward. Have the "manager" list at least five recommendations for communicating downward. Have everyone asterisk the one point on their lists they regard as most important. The pairs should then tell each other what they've asterisked.

4. Begin a round-robin of responses. Start with the "subordinates": have a "subordinate" stand and state his or her asterisked point. Call for immediate response: Do other class members think the recommendation is manipulative? How would they define "manipulative"? Could a given action be viewed as manipulative by one person and not by another? Do they endorse it? Would they use it?, et cetera. (**Note:** The response part of this exercise must move very quickly.) Then call on the second "subordinate" to give his or her most important point. Ask for input and then move on to the next. Continue until all the subordinates have had a chance to speak.

5. Continue the process by having each "manager" provide his or her most important point, followed by immediate and rapid feedback.

6. Show Transparency 35.1, *"Upward Communication,"* based on an article by William Tracey, president of Human Resources Enterprises of Cape Cod, Inc., who asserts that the key to effective boss management is communication. He gives these suggestions for prudent response when someone is being attacked by a boss or is simply in disagreement with a boss. Ask participants to comment on the ethical nature of the recommendations. Are there any with which participants disagree?

7. Debrief the exercise with a summary based on the Discussion questions.

Variation

Many of the understanding gaps between managers and employees can be closed by asking each to list their views on a certain issue. For example, the employee might list what he or she thinks is needed in order for him or her to be promoted. That employee's manager would make the same list. Then, the employee and his or her manager would meet to compare their lists, discuss the differences, and perhaps prioritize steps on a career path.

Discussion

➤ Is manipulation, like sexual harassment, determined by the recipient of such behavior or by the person engaged in the behavior?

➤ Under what conditions is manipulative behavior acceptable? (For example, parents often engage in such behavior with their children and vice versa. Is this acceptable? Why or why not?)

➤ If you realize an attempt at manipulation is being made, does the attempt then seem less offensive? Why or why not?

➤ What causes some people to be offended by such behavior and others to be not in the least affected by it?

Quotation

"Character is much easier kept than recovered."
–Thomas Paine

Points of Interest

Peter Belanger, president of Outbound Resources, Inc., of Van Nuys, California, endorses the concept of "conceding before continuing." He recognizes that in the minds of many, conceding is synonymous with failure or a loss of power. Yet, in an insightful contrarian view, he suggests backing off from a communication exchange. Such a tactic, he asserts, melts resistance and begins a relationship established on trust.

These are some of the phrases with which he concedes:

➤ "I don't think I can be of any help to you at all today."

➤ "Why don't I leave you alone for a few months?"

➤ "Sounds like you're up to your eyeballs in training already."

➤ "Your plate is full. Let me check back with you around (date) . . ."

UPWARD COMMUNICATION

- Never reply immediately.
- Ask for time to stop and think.
- Ask yourself what you want to happen.
- If time permits, rehearse your reply.
- Keep your voice soft.
- Ask the boss what he or she would like you to do.
- Listen to the response and repeat it.
- State what you want, but be willing to negotiate.
- Always let the boss have the last word.

—William Tracey, President, Human Resources Enterprises of Cape Cod, Inc.

ETHICAL MANAGEMENT

You Know
There's a Child

Approximately 20 minutes

Overview

Participants are asked to take a long and hard look at the elements within their workplace that constitute ethical management. Although the exercise begins on a lighthearted note, it quickly becomes a strong-headed compilation of ideas managers can incorporate into their own managerial style. The exercise concludes with a panel discussion.

Purpose

To compile a list of ways to demonstrate ethical management is being practiced.

Group Size

The group should be large enough to accommodate a panel presentation with at least six people in the audience to listen and interact with the panelists.

Room Arrangement

Arrange seating flexible enough to accommodate small groups and then a panel arrangement in the front of the room with the other seats arranged audience-style.

Materials

➤ Projector for transparencies or for PowerPoint slides
➤ Transparency 36.1, *"You know there's a child in the house if . . ."*

Procedure

1. Begin by showing Transparency 36.1. Ask for other examples that offer proof that a child or children live in a particular house.

2. Segue to the exercise by pointing out that ethical management—and unethical management as well—can be easily spotted by customers, subordinates, and senior managers alike.

3. Divide the group into smaller groups of three to five participants.

4. Have them list, as specifically as possible, actions and words that demonstrate a moral climate and those that evince breaches of ethics.

5. Ask each group to select a spokesperson to serve on a panel. The selection can be made in one of two ways: either the person who is most comfortable addressing a group can serve as spokesperson *or* the person who is *least* comfortable but who knows he or she needs to gain more experience.

6. Have the spokespersons come forward with their lists and form a panel, which you will moderate with these discussion questions and others if you wish. Involve the audience as much as possible.

Variation

The same construct ("You know there's a _____ in the organization if/when. . . .") may be used for Leadership, Coaching, Team-building, Supervision, and many other classes. The lists, once compiled, can be shared with future classes, published, and sent to participants' managers as an example of one of the instructional points made in the class.

Discussion

➤ Which is more powerful: truth or perception?

➤ To what extent are ethics truthfully manifested in your organization?

➤ To what extent does the perception of an ethical environment pervade the organization?

➤ Does your manager consciously think about creating an ethical environment?

➤ Does he or she think about creating the *appearance* of one?

➤ What evidence do you have of either the reality or the perception of reality, as far as an ethical culture is concerned?

Quotation

"I shall adopt new views as fast as they shall appear to be true views."
–Abraham Lincoln

Points of Interest

A survey conducted by the Ethics Resource Center in Washington, D.C. found that 60 percent of American companies have formal codes of ethics for doing business both domestically and abroad. Typically, these codes encompass the treatment of customers, suppliers, shareholders, employees, and the communities in which the firms are doing business.

You know there's a child in the house if . . .

you have to wash the soap before using it.

ETHICAL MANAGEMENT

Will the Real Ethical Manager Please Stand?

37

Approximately 25 minutes

Overview

This exercise attempts to close the gap between perception and reality by encouraging managers to assess themselves as they believe others see them and then to assess themselves as they see themselves.

Purpose

To develop awareness of the gap between perceptions of ethical behavior and the reality on which those perceptions are based.

Group Size

Any number of individuals can participate. Group members will first work alone and then in triads. (**Note:** This exercise works best with people who know each other well or participants who have worked together for most of the session. It's best not to use it early in the training day but rather after participants have had an opportunity to get to know one another.)

Room Arrangement

Arrange seating that can accommodate the formation of three-person subgroups.

Materials

Handout 37.1, *"Ethics Profile"* (**Note:** Each person should receive two copies: one to work on in class and the second to be taken back to the office, copied, and distributed to his or her staff.)

Procedure

1. Lead a brief discussion of the causes for discrepancies in the way we see ourselves and the way others see us. Some participants may be familiar with the Johari Window, with quadrants depicting what we know about ourselves, what others know about us, what we don't know about ourselves, and what others don't know about us. This could be used to illustrate the possible reasons for discrepancies. For example, if you know that you are rushing out of a building without stopping for pleasantries of any kind because you've just had a call that your child was injured, you could be regarded as purposeful. Those same actions, though, viewed by someone who didn't know your purpose, could be regarded as abrasive.

   You may also choose to note that words and actions are seldom regarded the same way by two different people. For example, prosecuting attorneys and defense attorneys present differing views of the same event—it's up to the jury to decide which presentation more accurately depicted the truth. And the jury's decision is not always the correct one. Fortunately or unfortunately, we live in a world of multiple interpretations for particular persons, places, and things.

2. Explain that you're going to distribute a self-assessment for the purpose of helping participants determine if a gap exists between their self-perception and the perception others may have of them.

3. Stress repeatedly that perceptions are not truth. If someone perceives managers in a more negative fashion than they perceive themselves, the other person is not necessarily right. The exercise is intended only to open dialogue, to explore why the difference might exist. It is not intended to label participants.

   Encourage participants to substantiate their answers if they can with specific references that may have led to their perceptions. This substantiation should be done both as they fill out the assessment individually, and then after, as they discuss it in triads.

4. Distribute the assessment form, Handout 37.1, *"Ethics Profile,"* and allow time for participants to complete it.

5. Form triads and encourage sensitive and supportive analyses and differences of opinion.

6. Ask each triad to characterize the nature of their discussions: For example, were they conducted in a professional, sensitive, nonthreatening manner? Were differences of opinion respectfully listened to? Were triad members interrupting one another? Were convincing examples presented? Did each person in the triad have an opportunity to contribute?

7. Debrief by asking one person in each triad to share his or her opinion of the way in which the triads discussed their responses.

8. Conclude with a strong recommendation that participants and managers use the form with their staff members and that they conduct subsequent discussions in the most professional manner possible.

Variation

Ideally, participants will take the assessment back to the workplace and make a copy for everyone whom they manage. To encourage honest responses, appoint one person to collect the completed (anonymous) surveys and to give them all at once to the manager. At a subsequent meeting (either one-on-one or with the staff as a whole), the manager—if he or she is brave enough—can stimulate dialogue regarding ways to improve.

Discussion

➤ What causes some people to wear "blinders" when it comes to their own behavior?

➤ Think of a time in your work life when someone misjudged you. Did he or she ever come to know the real you? What barriers were created by that incident?

➤ How often do you think the average person does an assessment of the way he or she sees himself or herself and of the way others see him or her?

Quotation

"Underpromise, overdeliver."
–Joel Pliskin

Points of Interest

Writing in *Executive Excellence,* Paul Evans, a professor of organizational behavior at INSEAD, maintains "Your assets are your potential liabilities."

Your successes lead to a predictable self-confidence. But excessive self-confidence, especially for those in authority, can lead a "pendulum swing toward failure."

Ethics Profile

DIRECTIONS

Actions, like most other things, are neutral in and of themselves. They can be executed, however, in an ethical or unethical manner; they can fall anywhere on the ethical continuum. Music, for example, is a neutral concept. When blasted 24/7, it can be torture for those in a prison camp. When performed harmoniously, it can provide an enchanted evening for hundreds of music lovers.

Look at the actions that you engage in as a manager. Consider how "socializing" might be unethical. For example, take a manager who spends a large portion of his or her time trying to fit in with executives, and barely deigns to say "good morning" to his or her subordinates. Clearly, this manager demonstrates little regard for the feelings of others. That same action, "socializing," though, could be regarded as a highly ethical behavior if a manager sought inclusion for all of his or her staff members and socialized with diverse employees or the newly hired or the less educated, to make them feel comfortable in the workplace.

Once you've thought about each item below, rate yourself on the ethical continuum by placing an "X" to show the manner in which you typically perform this action or the rationale behind your undertaking of this action. Consider genuine concern for others versus advancing your own cause or self-aggrandizing.

1.   **Socializing**

Shamefully Unethical   Extremely Ethical

---

2.   **Volunteering**

Shamefully Unethical   Extremely Ethical

---

3.   **Tolerating**

Shamefully Unethical   Extremely Ethical

4.　　　　　**Promoting the Department/Member**

Shamefully Unethical　　　　　　　　　　　　　　Extremely Ethical

5.　　　　　**Seeking Perfection**

Shamefully Unethical　　　　　　　　　　　　　　Extremely Ethical

6.　　　　　**Showing Sensitivity**

Shamefully Unethical　　　　　　　　　　　　　　Extremely Ethical

7.　　　　　**Achieving Goals**

Shamefully Unethical　　　　　　　　　　　　　　Extremely Ethical

8.　　　　　**Compromising**

Shamefully Unethical　　　　　　　　　　　　　　Extremely Ethical

9.　　　　　**Persuading**

Shamefully Unethical　　　　　　　　　　　　　　Extremely Ethical

10.　　　　　**Persisting**

Shamefully Unethical　　　　　　　　　　　　　　Extremely Ethical

38 Codified Ethics

Approximately 50 to 60 minutes

Overview

For those who manage employees but have not yet established a code of ethics, this exercise first asks participants to read a monograph regarding standards and then to incorporate specific values into a set of principles by which employees can interact honestly and respectfully.

Purpose

To create a set of ethical standards for use in the workplace.

Group Size

Any number of individuals can participate. Participants will first work alone and then in subgroups of three to five participants.

Room Arrangement

Arrange flexible seating that allows the formation of subgroups.

Materials

Handout 38.1, Monograph: *"Integrity Gauges"*

Procedure

1. Introduce the activity by asking if anyone has a special ethical principle—such as "Do unto others as you would have others do unto you"—that governs everyday behavior. Briefly discuss these and then explain that they'll be working today to prepare a set of such principles for the workplace.

2. Distribute Handout 38.1, Monograph: *"Integrity Gauges."* Allow at least 10 minutes for participants to read "Integrity Gauges." Encourage them to underline points they find interesting and to write questions and comments in the margins. Point out that a code of ethics can take many forms: a series of words (Pride, Passion, Perfection) or a series of sentences or even a series of questions.

3. Ask them to take 5 minutes to review their underlinings/notes and to formulate a set of ethical principles, simply stated, to govern interactions in the workplace. (Encourage originality. Ideally, their principles will not sound like the questions posed in the monograph-handout.)

4. Form subgroups of three or four and have participants discuss the questions in the handout. They will need about 15 minutes to do this.

5. Then, each person in the subgroup will share the set of ethical principles he or she created. The group will take another 10 minutes for this sharing/discussion.

6. Once they've had a chance to hear and think about several sets of ethical principles for the workplace, they will next formulate one synthesized set of statements. (Their statements could be in the form of declarative or interrogative statements.)

7. Ask a spokesperson from each subgroup to leave the room with the list of his or her group's synthesized principles. In a breakout room (or a corner of the classroom, if no other room is available), ask the subgroup representatives to collaborate to produce one comprehensive list that would serve in any workplace.

8. As they do so, guide a discussion with the remaining participants, using the Discussion questions, Quotation, and/or Points of Interest as guideposts. Ask them to relate, for example, the six considerations cited by Frisch in the Points of Interest to the implementation of a new ethics policy in their own organizations.

9. Bring closure to the exercise by having a spokesperson from the group composed of subgroup representatives report on their work.

Variation

If the group is willing to have their work made public, ask for a volunteer to obtain permission from management to have these principles printed and distributed throughout the organization.

Assign different subgroups different sections of the monograph so that subsequent reports can be made on the monograph as a whole.

Discussion

> What principles that you acquired during childhood still guide you today?

> Do you think America has become a "kinder, gentler" nation since President George H. Bush first hoped we could, more than a decade ago?

> In your opinion, what ethical guidelines govern your organization's treatment of employees, customers, and others directly or indirectly affected by the product or service you provide?

Quotation

"We are what we repeatedly do. Excellence, then, is not an act, but a habit."
–Aristotle

Points of Interest

Gerald Frisch, president of GFA, Inc., and managing director of the National Cost Reduction Institute, recommends policy-implementers first consider six areas before they attempt to establish a new policy, such as a code of ethics for everyone to follow:

> The Big Picture
> History
> Memory
> Conferences
> Dialogue
> Payoff

Integrity Gauges

Most people know when they are manipulative and when they are being manipulated. Nonetheless, neither families, schools, nor businesses can operate on the assumption that individuals will recognize manipulation when they use it and when it is being used on them. It is much better to have a clearly articulated set of principles for the ethical conduct of family affairs, school practices, and business operations. Two questions precede the asking of questions that will lead to the formation of ethical guidelines: Can we agree that we need a code of ethics? If you and/or the group with whom you are interacting answer yes, then the next question is: Are we willing to develop that code?

In a sense, the macrocosmic code of ethics is like the microcosmic set of ground rules that governs team meetings. Based on integrity, honor, and respect, the code of ethics should clearly stipulate what is proper and what will not be tolerated in various circumstances. Many find a set of standard questions can help guide employees. Encourage your staff to ask questions such as these, developed in 1932, by businessman Herbert J. Taylor. They represent a four-way test to evaluate intended actions:

➤ Is it the truth?

➤ Is it fair to all concerned?

➤ Will it build goodwill and better friendships?

➤ Will it be beneficial to all concerned?

In keeping with such interrogative introspections, these are but a few of the additional questions that can help you to create a code of ethical behavior:

➤ Could this harm us in any way?

➤ Could it harm others?

➤ Is it legal?

➤ Does it feel wrong?

➤ If the customer could see us doing this, would he or she be willing to pay for it?

(continued)

- ➤ Would I still do this if news of it were broadcast in tomorrow's newspaper?
- ➤ Would we be proud to do this with our families watching?
- ➤ Who will be the primary beneficiary of this action? The secondary beneficiary?
- ➤ Are there safety, union, or OSHA issues we may have overlooked?
- ➤ What actions would constitute violations of ethical conduct?
- ➤ What are the consequences of violations?
- ➤ In what ways might we be, even unknowingly, pressuring others to act unethically?
- ➤ How do we maintain quality when we have to do more with less?
- ➤ In different circumstances (transculturally, for example), how might our tolerance limits change?
- ➤ Should we consider creating hot lines or an ombudsman position?
- ➤ How and how often should the code be disseminated?
- ➤ What complex or confusing situations might make our ethical guidelines murky in the eyes of some?
- ➤ What could cause confidence to be shattered?
- ➤ Does this action advance our mission?
- ➤ Is this action in keeping with our values?
- ➤ Would we be proud to say afterward that we were a part of this action?
- ➤ What assurances could we give regarding possible outcomes?
- ➤ Could we be rewarding unethical behavior in any way?
- ➤ What could we point to in the past that shows we have an ethical track record?
- ➤ What ethical messages are we sending or failing to send to others?
- ➤ Do people know what to do or to whom to turn if they have concerns about ethical conduct?
- ➤ If we could develop an intranet message regarding integrity, what would it say?

ETHICAL MANAGEMENT

Stand Up for Standards

Mike Morrell

Approximately 60 minutes

Overview

This exercise enables managers to explore their own ethical standards on a particular issue and to compare them to those of their colleagues. They may subsequently decide to adjust their own standards on the basis of this comparison.

Purpose

➤ To develop awareness of ethical standards—one's own as well as those of colleagues.

➤ To engage participants in the learning process known as peer learning.

Group Size

Any number of individuals can participate. The group should be divided into subgroups of four or five.

Room Arrangement

Ideally, arrange table groups that accommodate four or five participants.

Materials

➤ Flipchart and marking pens

➤ Handout 39.1, *"Ethical Issues"*

Procedure

1. Introduce the purpose of the exercise, viz., to develop awareness of ethical standards.

2. Briefly discuss the meaning of Emerson's quotation, *"A foolish consistency is the hobgoblin of little minds."* Discuss the importance of *not* remaining consistent over an entire lifetime. Explore how and why and when values undergo shifts—for example, as a teen-ager, you may have empathized with Romeo and Juliet and the value they placed on love. As a parent, however, you may be more inclined to view the love story from a parent's perspective and might, thus, value life over love. Segue to the hope that participants will remain open to ideas that may conflict with their own.

3. Ask the group for suggestions about ethical quandaries that managers often have to face. List these on chart paper. If no suggestions are forthcoming, write up your own list. Suggestions follow.

   ➤ Hiring based on "who you know" rather than "what you know."

   ➤ Using paid time for private phone calls, Internet, e-mails, et cetera.

   ➤ Putting pressure on employees to work overtime, weekends, et cetera to meet client workload.

   ➤ Permitting "different strokes for different folks" or treating everyone the same.

   ➤ Wining and dining clients: What's acceptable? What's not? Why not?

   ➤ Bending the rules for special circumstances: death in the family, prolonged illness, et cetera.

   ➤ Taking responsibility for employee welfare.

   ➤ Facilitating employee career development. (How far should this extend outside the current company career path?)

   ➤ Communicating honestly: To what extent are "white lies" or "sins of omission" acceptable? Toward employees? Toward clients?

4. Ask participants to vote on the issue (or issues, depending on the time allowed) that interest them most. Tally the votes and record the numbers next to each item on the flipchart.

5. Next, form discussion subgroups based on their selections. Those who voted for the first item, for example, would constitute the first group, and so on.

6. Give each group Handout 39.1, *"Ethical Issues,"* and sufficient time to complete it—at least 30 minutes.

7. Bring the subgroups back together and let each in turn present its findings.

8. Highlight the differences in the standards of different individuals.

9. Lead a discussion regarding the causes of the differences. Determine, if possible, if the differences are acceptable in the organizational culture or climate.

10. Ask participants to share the extent to which the exercise influenced them.

11. Bring closure by asking each person to tell if his or her standards were altered at all after listening to colleagues' viewpoints. (If the group is large, allow time for subgroup discussion and then ask a spokesperson from each subgroup to present a synopsis.)

Variation

Ask everyone to think about a workplace issue involving ethics and to write his or her position regarding this issue on a scrap of paper. (For example: the issue of using company equipment for personal use or engaging in rumors or deliberately making false promises during the hiring process.) Call on five people (assuming a class size of 25) to stand and state their positions. Then ask the remaining participants to join one of the five groups that each of the five volunteers will lead. Participants should make their selection on the basis of their own feelings (of agreement or disagreement) regarding the positions taken by the five volunteers.

Allow the subgroups time to explore one another's viewpoint but also to achieve consensus, if they can, on a corporate position that should be taken regarding this particular issue.

DISCUSSION

➤ To what extent does the organization have the right to regulate personal freedom issues, such as groups of employees speaking a language other than English or the primary language in your workplace if it is not English?

➤ Could it be dangerous to open certain topics to discussion? If so, how? Which topics? How are they dangerous?

➤ What current events may have or should have influenced your own organization's ethics policy?

Quotation

"Questions focus our thinking. Ask empowering questions like 'What's good about this?' 'What's not perfect about it yet?' 'What am I going to do next time?' 'How can I do this and have fun doing it?'"
–Charles Connolly

Points of Interest

The sample issue of _Positive Leadership_ provides an ethical checklist, consisting of questions to help in the formation of both individual and organizational ethics policies.

➤ Is it legal?

➤ Is it fair and balanced?

➤ How will I feel when it's done?

MIKE enjoys the process of discovering what it means to be a human being. He sees organizations and organizational development as the product of—and the current environment for—the further development of and interplay between individuals. He facilitates both organizational and individual staff development in the roles of trainer, coach, consultant, and change manager.

Ethical Issues

1. Specify an ethical issue you are facing at work; tell how important it is, and give a few examples of situations in which it is relevant.

   _____

   _____

2. Describe what your own ethical stance is with respect to this issue and compare this with any formal policy that you are aware of.

   _____

   _____

3. Describe how you adhere to your own ethical standards for this issue.

   _____

   _____

4. Describe the influence you have over others in regards to this issue. How do you use this ability to influence?

   _____

   _____

5. Discuss the differences with other members of the subgroup on points (1) to (4).

   _____

   _____

6. Once the differences have been noted, work to develop a cohesive statement that represents both similarities and differences. A spokesperson will present your group's results at the plenary session.

   _____

   _____

Perform as a Norm

M. Vasudevan

Approximately 45 to 60 minutes

Overview

Designed to boost performance levels, this exercise encourages participants to consider simple, workable, and nonmanipulative ways to remove performance blocks and to develop employees' full potential.

Purpose

➤ To acquaint participants with positive tools for narrowing the gap between task demands and available (or assumed to be unavailable) resources.

➤ To effect realization that fear is a negative and sometimes unethical way to motivate employees.

Group Size

Any number of individuals can participate. The group should be divided into subgroups of four or five.

Room Arrangement

If possible, arrange table groups for four or five participants each.

Materials

➤ Flipchart and marking pens

➤ Projector for transparencies or for PowerPoint slides

➤ Transparency 40.1, *"The Walk"*

➤ Transparency 40.2, *"The Jump"*

➤ Transparency 40.3, *"The Leap"*

➤ Transparency 40.4, *"The Motivation"*

Procedure

1. Begin by narrating the story of Tenali Rama and the Royal Banquet, as follows:

   Krishna Deva Raya, famous king of Vijaynagar (a powerful south Indian Empire of the 15th century), devised a test of his courtiers' resourcefulness. He invited them all to a grand banquet at the palace. Raya received the guests himself on the appointed day, and before leading them in to the banquet hall—all readied with rows of ornate chairs and silver plates and goblets—he laid down a seemingly small condition. The guests were to partake of the feast without flexing their elbows! The puzzled guests thought this a cruel joke and were about to turn away, clearly crestfallen, when the ever-resourceful Tenali Rama (the chief courtier and the king's confidant) came up with a workable solution that enabled them all to enjoy the banquet.

2. Ask the group members to discuss a possible solution to the problem. Record their responses on a flipchart.

3. Share the solution: If each guest fed the guest to his or her left, none would have to bend his or her elbows. Discuss the answers from the perspective of practicality.

4. Emphasize the point that Tenali Rama succeeded by adapting to the awkward condition imposed by the king.

5. Conclude by pointing out that a shortfall between allocated resources and task demands is best bridged by adaptation, that is, matching changes in operational conditions with suitable modifications in operational methods.

   Use these classic examples:

   ➤ Napoleon Bonaparte, when asked how he responded to unfavorable circumstances, replied, *"Unfavorable circumstances? Why, I always make my own circumstances and I never make them unfavorable."* To be sure, he kept his adversaries at bay by making suitable and necessary changes in his own strategies. He provides an excellent example of adapting to changing task demands.

   ➤ In World War II, bomber pilots learned to neutralize the newly developed RADAR tracking system, just by going out of range and flying at treetop level. They used ingenuity to adapt to this potential threat of detection.

Variation

Relate the discussion of task demands and available or assumed-to-be-unavailable resources to the following experience the author of this exercise had.

Once, sitting in his parked car on the roadside adjacent to an irrigation ditch, he saw a youngster and an old man (perhaps the grandfather) walking along the ditch on the far side of the road. (Display Transparency 40.1 at this point.) *At a narrow point of the ditch, the boy jumped across and waited for the old man to do likewise.* (Show Transparency 40.2 at this point.) *But the old man stayed on his side and pointed to the stone slab across the ditch, a little way off. The old man said he thought it would be safer to use the slab than to jump over. After a couple of steps, however, the old man hitched up his dhothi (loincloth) and took a flying leap over the ditch.* (Display Transparency 40.3.)

Ask the group to discuss why the old man suddenly changed his mind. Have the groups note their answers in a few words on slips of paper. You can read these aloud and then lead a group discussion that compares their answers to this one (illustrated by showing Transparency 40.4).

Answer: The physical capacity for leaping lay dormant in the old man, hidden under the imagined infirmities of old age. It came alive only when the motivation was provided by a rushing bull. The magic of motivation is that it unlocks dormant potential. All feats of mankind over the ages have been primed by motivation—whether those feats are accomplished by a single individual or by an entire team.

It is not likely that any group realized a charging bull could bring out potential the old man didn't even realize he had. But, if a group did realize this possibility, they are to be applauded.

Discussion

➤ What's the best way for a manager to motivate his or her staff?

➤ Is fear ever appropriate as a motivational tool? If so, under what circumstances?

Quotation

"The first problem for all of us, men and women, is not to learn, but to unlearn."
–Gloria Steinem

Points of Interest

The story of the Yuks illustrates the need for caution when unleashing positive and powerful forces within the workplace. (It *is* possible to have too much of a good thing.) Sugar cane beetles were destroying the crops in Australia until scientists introduced a unique toad, nicknamed the "Yuk." Balance in the ecosystem was to have been achieved when the yuks destroyed the beetles and allowed the vegetation to thrive. Instead, the yuks thrived. They had no natural enemies and in time became more of a threat to the environment than the original beetles were.

The phenomenon has since come to be called the "yuk effect" and pertains to the downside of positive change.

M. VASUDEVAN, Indian Institute of Science, Bangalore. Mr. Vasudevan has been a votary of maximizing efficiency in all spheres of human endeavor, with the aim of improving the welfare of humanity. He is a freelance writer and speaker on practical ways to boost productivity and has been the recipient of the State Government Award (from Karnataka State Government, in recognition of contributions in the field of Social Service) in 1991 and the National Award (from the Ministry of Social Welfare, in recognition of Outstanding Efficiency) in 1984.

"The Walk"

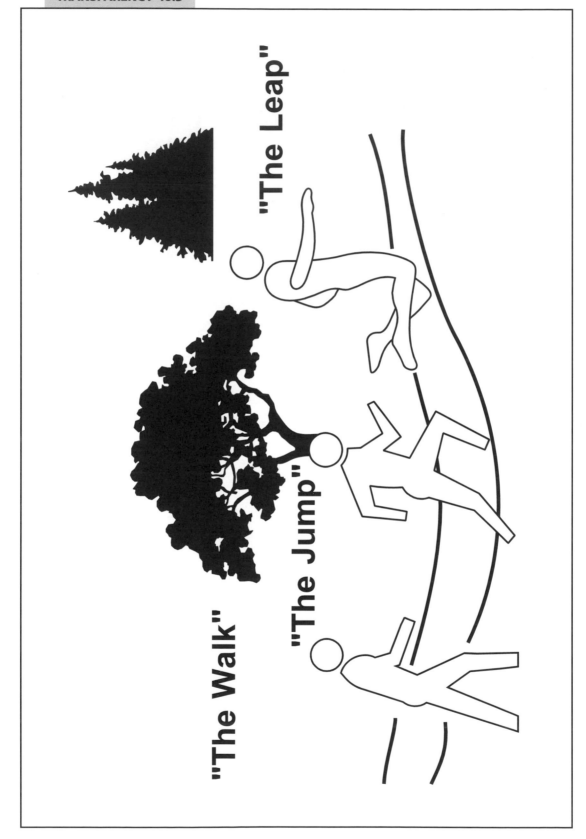

"The Leap"

"The Walk"

"The Jump"

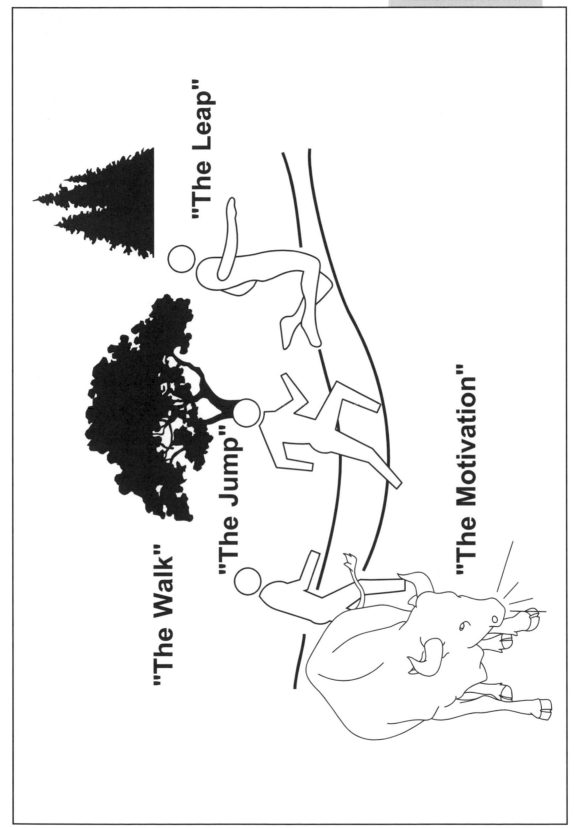

Ethical Teamwork

Ethical Teamwork

KRISTIN J. ARNOLD

The very essence of teams and teamwork is to seek common ground and search for "the truth."

Gone unstated, individual team members create their own definitions of "the truth," what's right and wrong, as well as their own interpretations of proper standards of behavior. When team members are operating from different truths, assumptions, and values, teams invariably are rife with conflict, behave badly, and are simply nonproductive.

When team members are in alignment with the same values and standards, you don't have these kinds of problems. They are open to different points of view. Extraordinary teams work together to discover the truth, searching for common ground and building a consensus.

More importantly, they invest time to discuss and explicitly define their standards—or how they will work together to achieve "the truth." Some call these standards "ground rules," "guiding principles," or "team norms." They are explicit agreements on how the team will function. They clearly articulate boundaries of appropriate behavior. Effective ground rules *prevent* undesirable behaviors from happening in the first place. They also create a space to *intervene* gracefully—reminding each other of the prior agreements made.

As you formulate your ground rules, consider how your team will deal with common concerns such as:

> **Interruptions.** What to do when team members are called out of the meeting. How will you deal with phone calls and messages? Will pager and cellular phones be tolerated?

> **Assignments.** If team members cannot fulfill their obligations, who should they notify and by when?

> **Substitutions.** In the event a team member can't make it to the meeting, are "substitutions" allowed? How will the team's work be communicated to the missing team member?

> **Decisions.** How will the team make decisions? Are team members aiming for consensus? Is there a "fallback" in case the team can't come to a consensus? Is the team leader ultimately responsible for making the decision?

➤ **Confidentiality.** Are there topics or kinds of information that should not be discussed outside the team?

➤ **Penalties.** How will the team deal with minor and chronic violations to the ground rules?

Ground rules are simply the glue that holds the team together. Here's an example of one extraordinary team's ground rules:

➤ **Honor time limits.** Be on time. Start on time. End on time. Set a time frame for each deliverable. Do your part to meet individual and team commitments.

➤ **All participate ... no one dominates.** Ask for ideas from everyone. Recognize and consider others' ideas. Accept all suggestions as valid for consideration.

➤ **Work together.** Team members communicate and work closely together and make every effort to support one another. Keep one another informed. Work together to solve problems. Offer help without being asked.

➤ **Listen as allies.** Give your undivided attention to the person speaking. Try to understand others first; second, try to be understood. Respect each other by not interrupting. Stay on track. Stick to the subject at hand. Minimize distractions and needless debate.

➤ **Be considerate.** Consider the background, motivations, and skills of other team members when offering help or advice. Be open to constructive feedback.

➤ **Celebrate small successes.** Recognize team and individual effort.

➤ **Aim for consensus.** But if we cannot agree, we will park the issue on a "logjam" lot for a specified period of time.

➤ **Knock three times.** Simply knock your knuckle or a pen on the table three times if the discussion starts to wander or there is another minor violation of the ground rules. Whoever is speaking should stop and refocus on the topic.

➤ **Respect time and each other.**

It all boils down to this one last ground rule: respect each other. When you respect each other, it is much easier to discover the truth.

KRISTIN J. ARNOLD, CPCM, helps corporations, government, and nonprofit organizations achieve extraordinary results. With years of team-building and facilitation experience, Kristin specializes in coaching executives and their leadership, management, and employee teams, particularly in the areas of strategic, business, and project planning; process improvement; decision-making; and collaborative problem-solving.

In addition to facilitation services, QPC, Inc., offers diversified programs around the team concept to meet the needs of CEOs, COOs, executives, managers, and team members. Her highly customized speeches and seminars are instrumental in achieving higher performance and results within the workplace.

ETHICAL TEAMWORK

Blindfold Obstacle Course

Stephen Hobbs

Approximately 60 to 75 minutes

Overview

This exercise highlights the value of trustworthiness as it affects various roles and tactics team members use to deal with a perceived stressful situation. While the main activity may be made as easy or difficult as required, careful observation during the exercise and skillful facilitation by an experienced trainer during the debriefing is required. The exercise may be conducted in a large space, either indoors or outdoors.

Purpose

To develop awareness of the need for trust among team members.

Group Size

The group should be large enough to have two equal-sized teams of at least five participants, plus an observer and guide for each team.

Room Arrangement

A large area (indoors or out) is required.

Materials

➤ Blindfolds for each participating team member
➤ One rope per team long enough to tie each participant to other team members in a row with 2 to 3 feet of rope between each person. (The rope length will be approximately 6 feet times the number of participants.)

➤ Obstacles for the groups to go over, under, through, and/or around

➤ Clipboards and pencils for observers (There will be one observer per team)

➤ Handout 41.1, *Observation Sheet* (one for each observer)

➤ Suggested Obstacles

Inside Room

➤ Two sturdy tables to go over, under, or through

➤ Ropes tied between four to eight solid stands to act as a "hallway" to follow

➤ Ropes tied between two solid stands for teams to go under or to serve as "electric" fences

➤ Two to four plastic sheets taped to the ground to signify water obstacles

Outside Room

➤ Two sturdy tables, for example, picnic tables to go over, under, or through

➤ Ropes tied between three to five trees to act as a "hallway" to follow (**Note:** If trees are within a few yards of each other, use five. If the trees are separated by at least 5 yards, use three trees.)

➤ Ropes tied between two trees for teams to go under or to serve as "electric" fences

➤ Actual water hazards, for example, slow moving creeks, shallow ponds, puddles

Procedure

1. Divide participants into equal-sized groups, no larger than eight participants per group.

2. Assign one observer and one guide per group. Observers are responsible for completing Handout 41.1, *Observation Sheet*, and providing observations to the group during the activity debriefing. Guides are responsible for ensuring their assigned group completes the exercise safely. Each observer receives an observer sheet, clipboard, and pencil.

3. Give each group a rope and blindfold for every person (excluding the guide and the observer). They are instructed

to tie themselves together in a row, then place the blindfolds over their eyes so they are not able to see.

4. The guide from each group leads the group to their designated starting point and stays with them for the duration of the blindfold exercise. Guides tell their group what obstacle they are about to negotiate, for example, a "water" obstacle, an "electric" fence, a rope hallway, et cetera.

5. With assistance from their guides, teams have 5 minutes to negotiate the obstacles.

6. At the end of 5 minutes, the observer selects the team member who has been the least involved in the process to become the new guide. The original guide becomes a member of the blindfolded team. While still blindfolded, the team must reorder and retie themselves to include the new member.

7. The new group has 5 minutes to continue negotiating the remaining obstacles.

8. When the next 5-minute time frame is over, group members remove their blindfolds and untie themselves. Each group, including the observers and guides, gather around a flipchart and choose a scribe who writes the answers to the following questions:

   ➤ Describe the experience in adjectives, for example, "exciting," "scary," "frustrating."

   ➤ What is the effect of trust involved in the activity on a team?

   ➤ What did you learn about your team?

   ➤ What did you learn about the roles each team member takes on?

   ➤ What did you learn about the roles you take on within the team?

9. The observer shares his or her observations (based on what has been written on the Observation Sheets) after answers to the above questions are given.

10. Each group has a spokesperson to report answers to the questions in step 8 to the larger group.

11. Based on the ideas shared, debrief the exercise from a larger viewpoint, identifying team issues raised, "food for thought"

for participants' return to the workplace, and possible next steps toward establishing and maintaining their team. Discuss the obstacle course as a metaphor for workplace barriers and how teams must rely on one another to overcome these barriers.

12. Debrief with a short lecture on trust, summarizing the points made in step 8. The following concepts/questions could be included:

Trust is manifested in four ways:

Contract . . . you agree to do what you said you would do by shaking hands or signing a contract.

Competency . . . you have the capabilities to accomplish the task.

Intentionality . . . you will fulfill your obligations (meet the goals and objectives) until the task is finished.

Depth . . . you will finish the task at a level consistent with what is defined as "good work" in relation to the task.

1. What was the contract among members—that is, what did they agree to do? (Relate discussion to written and unwritten contracts that guide us in the workplace.)

2. What were the competencies (such as leadership, creativity) shown as they planned to overcome obstacles? (Relate discussion to qualities we expect from organizational and governmental leaders.)

3. What intentions (pertaining to goals, safety, leadership, et cetera) were associated with this activity? (Relate discussion to the gap between intention and actualization of workplace mission or to the reasons why best workplace intentions sometimes go astray.)

4. What depth of completion was there? How closely was the intended plan followed? (Relate the discussion to the ethics of cutting corners in the workplace or failing to provide complete quality because of pressure to get the job done.)

5. Trustworthiness is realized through truthfulness or honesty, sincerity, candor, integrity, promise-keeping, loyalty. Of these principles, which were apparent in the activity? (Relate discussion to trust levels in participants' workplaces.)

Note that these same questions can be asked in the workplace every day.

STEPHEN HOBBS, ED.D., is the creator of the WELLTH Learning Network, Inc., and co-founder of The International Institute for Cultural Transition, Inc., and the Cultural Transition Institute. His work experience includes manager, consultant, instructor, facilitator, theorist, and published author. His practice focuses on customized experience-based learning adventures for individuals, groups, and teams; culture and transition; workplace learning; and the manager as educator.

DENISE DOLPH is the president of Co-Creations, Inc., and is an associate of the WELLTH Learning Network. She is a seasoned human resources generalist with specialization in training and development, career consulting, and recruitment.

Observation Sheet

1. How did the team determine the order of the group when tying themselves together?

   _____

   _____

2. How did the team determine which team members would be the leader?

   _____

   _____

3. What roles did the other team members take?

   _____

   _____

4. Who gave the other team members verbal and physical assistance through the obstacles?

   _____

   _____

5. Did the role of leader change throughout the exercise? If so, what caused the change?

   _____

   _____

6. How did the team determine how to negotiate each obstacle?

   _____

   _____

7. Did each group work collaboratively or competitively with other groups during the exercise? How did they determine if they would be collaborative or competitive?

   _____

   _____

8. What issues were raised during the exercise, for example, trust, leadership, conflict?

   _____

   _____

ETHICAL TEAMWORK

Cosmetic or Cosmological?

Approximately 45 minutes

Overview

The issue of spending training dollars wisely appears in this case study, which has team members share their views on popular courses of team action.

Purpose

➤ To encourage honest and full disclosure regarding team choices and decisions.

➤ To stimulate thinking about in-depth alternatives to expensive team-building programs.

Group Size

Any number of individuals can participate. Participants will work in teams of five to six.

Room Arrangement

If possible, arrange round table groupings for team meetings.

Materials

➤ Flipchart and marking pens

➤ Handout 42.1, *Cotton Candy Case Study*

Procedure

1. Begin the activity by sharing Bob Root's comment in an interview with Mark McMaster. (Root is managing director of Orion Learning International, which facilitates team-building programs for organizations.) "People have a sense of concern not only because of the state of the economy but also for their own job security. The recent [corporate] scandals only increase the need for more dialogue."

2. Lead a 5- to 10-minute discussion by asking:

➤ How concerned are you about the economy?

➤ How concerned are you about losing your job?

➤ To what extent have recent corporate scandals affected you?

➤ Do you feel a need for more dialogue with your organization's leaders?

➤ Do you feel trust has eroded in your workplace between managers and their staffs?

➤ What do you feel is the best way to restore trust—either in your own organization or in other organizations— where trust levels have declined?

3. Divide the group into teams of five or six participants. Ask them to take about 10 minutes to brainstorm ideas regarding the last question concerning ways to restore trust.

4. Call on a spokesperson from each team to read the group's list of recommendations. If and when reference is made to off-site team-building programs such as ropes courses or sailing excursions, note the recommendation on the flipchart.

If no such references were made, ask why not. List some of the reasons on the flipchart and ask for further input from the whole group regarding the validity of the reasons provided. If some subgroups did list off-site programs as a way to restore trust, ask the group at large what their experiences have been with such programs.

5. After a 5- to 10-minute discussion in step 4, introduce Stephen Covey's observation from the Quotation section, in which he likens some team-building programs to cotton candy. Open his remarks to further discussion. Then take about 5 minutes to list—with input from the entire group—trust-building, team-building activities that might be substituted for such programs. Suggest activities such as building a Habitat for Humanity. Such no-cost efforts not only have an ethical purpose but also develop teamwork via interdependency and shared problem-solving. In addition, they are more cosmological than cosmetic in their impact.

6. Distribute Handout 42.1, *"Cotton Candy Case Study."* Allow approximately 5 minutes for the same subgroups to work on the questions listed in the handout.

7. Conclude the activity by calling on a spokesperson from each team to answer one question each from the case study handout. If there are more questions than teams, continue in a round-robin fashion until all the questions have been answered. Provide input on each response to tie together the comments and the purpose of the exercise—to encourage complete input from all team members and to find inexpensive but far-reaching ways to develop team trust (Allow at least 5 minutes for this final step.)

Variation

Obtain in advance information regarding involvement in humanitarian projects, such as Habitat for Humanity. Provide copies of requirements or goals different projects might have and ask groups to devise a plan of action that will help them engage in team-building efforts that are less cosmetic, less expensive, yet more ethically important than sending team members off to resorts, retreats, or cruises.

Ask participants to compile ideas that will benefit others, develop teamwork, and minimize expenditures. For example, the team appoints one person to be the collector of loose change. He or she is responsible for asking team members at the end of the work week to donate all their loose change. The money is then used to sponsor an impoverished child in a foreign country. The Save-the-Children foundation is but one of many that will arrange for your team to make a big change in a little person's life: 800-243-5075. The monies go toward community development, helping families to help themselves. The team can correspond with the child they are helping and will receive an annual progress report on the developmental activities. Each team member can take on the additional responsibility of inspiring other workplace teams to undertake these virtual adoptions.

Discussion

➤ Is there a correlation between an individual's "cheating" on the golf course and that same individual's behavior at work? By extension, can a given team act both ethically and unethically in two different situations?

➤ Why or when could it be wrong, or even unethical, to voice your opinion regarding a team's intended course of action?

➤ What might be the down side of sending an executive team off for a week at DisneyWorld or off on a team-building cruise?

➤ Should managers and employees serve on the same teams?

➤ What are the advantages and disadvantages to training that involves off-site team-building ventures?

➤ Other than these ventures, how can teams develop respectful co-dependency?

Quotation

"A lot of team-building programs are very cosmetic. It's a lot like cotton candy—it tastes good, but doesn't nourish the organization in a way that allows it to explore its deeper issues."
—Stephen Covey

Points of Interest

The St. Louis-based consulting firm of Watson Wyatt found that fewer than 40% of people trust executive leaders in American firms. The number who expressed confidence in the job being done by their own leaders didn't even reach 50%. Only 63% felt confident that their own organizations were operating with honesty and integrity. (It would be interesting to poll the group on these points and see how the percentages compare with the national figures cited here. Ask what is being done (in addition to or in place of trust-buidling and team-building endeavors) to restore confidence in their firm.

Cotton Candy Case Study

SITUATION

Jennifer Donnelly serves on a management team struggling to maintain a positive attitude—not only toward the project they have been assigned but also toward the organization itself. A high-level executive was recently replaced after reporters discovered he had lied about having earned an MBA and the stain of his unethical behavior is spreading in several directions.

In an effort to restore trust, the executive's successor has proposed sending the team for a 4-day team-building program, to be held on a golf course in the Southwest.

Jennifer, a task-oriented individual who does not play golf, is opposed to the idea. She acknowledges there is a problem with trust in the organization but suspects that the off-site retreat will seem like a "mini-vacation" to others. She also fears more time will be spent on the golf course than in a meeting room, working on the serious issues that face the team.

Unfortunately, Jennifer is new to the team and not as experienced as the more veteran team members. She fears her opinion is a singular one, and so has decided not to voice her objections.

Your team is to discuss the all the questions that follow and will share one in particular with the group at large.

1. What's the best way for a team to elicit honest opinions from each of its group members?

   _____

   _____

   _____

   _____

(continued)

2. Just as there as sins of omission and sins of commission, some might feel it is wrong (possibly unethical) of Jennifer not to share her true feelings on this issue. Would you agree?

_____

_____

_____

_____

3. What would be the pros and the cons of having the newly hired executive present at the meeting when the golf-resort question will be decided upon?

_____

_____

_____

_____

4. What other forums (e.g., a "town hall") and methods (e.g., anonymous votes with rationale) could be employed to obtain the full and direct honest responses of team members?

_____

_____

_____

_____

5. What negative consequences (if only in the form of rumors) might be engendered if the decision is made to proceed with what some call "cotton candy" training (namely, team-building retreats in lush settings)?

_____

_____

_____

_____

ETHICAL TEAMWORK

Judgment Daze

Approximately 45 minutes

Overview

Teams discuss their reasons for selecting possible courses of action related to actual work-related cases. The team(s) that most often rules the way the judge ruled is awarded a token prize.

Purpose

To apprise participants of legal outcomes that may prevent them from engaging in unethical behavior.

Group Size

A group of any size will work, as long as teams can be formed with the same number of participants in each.

Room Arrangement

Arrange seating that will accommodate teams working around a table.

Materials

➤ Handouts 43.1 through 43.5, *"Court Shorts,"* for each participant

➤ **Optional:** Token prizes for the winning team, such as miniature gavels or simply pieces of fruit or books about teamwork

Procedure

1. Discuss the fact that laws are broken sometimes by people who are absolutely unaware that the laws they are breaking even exist. In fact, team members may be unaware of some laws that could directly affect teams in the workplace.

2. Present an overview of the assignment: Teams will discuss workplace situations involving teams and team members and will come to decisions regarding the "right" course of action.

The team that has the most right answers will emerge victorious and will be so recognized (if only through applause).

3. Divide the group into teams with an equal number of participants in each.

4. Distribute the first handout and allow the teams 5 minutes to complete it.

5. Continue with each of the remaining handouts.

6. Share the answers:

1 = False. If such remarks are made in the presence of employees likely to take offense at such statements, Ken may be guilty of unlawful harassment.

2 = True. But an employee who claimed he had taped conversations without telling people just to refresh his memory had to pay co-workers and his company $132,000.

3 = True (assuming this was not a singular example). In the actual case, a New York City bank had to pay the employee $2,600,000.

4 = True. The law firm in the actual case had to pay a $6,900,000 fine and the attorney himself (who was also guilty of touching the employee and making lewd remarks) was fined $225,000.

5 = False. The court found "the First Amendment is not a license for interference with the proper functioning of the workplace." The court also denied the discrimination claim as the company was able to prove its policies applied to everyone.

7. Award recognition and possibly token prizes to the winning team(s).

Variation

Invite someone from the legal department of the participants' organization (or another organization) to discuss labor and employment laws.

Discussion

➤ What is the worst legal mistake you can make at work?

➤ How much training has been provided regarding legislation pertaining to family leave, for example, or harassment? How could teams learn more about laws that may affect them?

➤ How much responsibility does or should your organization assume in making employees aware of labor and employment laws?

Quotation

_____

"Leadership is a potent combination of strategy and character. But if you must be without one, be without the strategy."
—General H. Norman Schwarzkopf

Points of Interest

_____

When infractions have occurred, it's the team leader's or supervisor's responsibility to provide coaching feedback to the person who may have committed the infraction. The following questions will help during coaching sessions:

1. Is there a real infraction or simply hearsay evidence of such?

2. Have standards been made clear to the individual before the incident?

3. Can you assume the correct behavior would be "obvious" to any reasonable person?

4. Has such behavior been tolerated in the past?

5. Has tolerance of the behavior been accepted in the past depending on the individual, the group, the task, and the situation?

6. Will you be able to maintain your objectivity in this investigation?

7. What resources do you need to call on?

8. Should there be a suspension period for the employee while the investigation is ongoing?

9. Have you given the employee an opportunity to present his or her version of the event?

10. What disciplinary precedents are there?

11. What does the employee's previous record tell you?

12. Could the contemplated action be considered discriminatory?

13. What documentation is required? How much time is needed to resolve this issue?

14. What possible repercussions could be harmful to others? To the organization itself?

Court Shorts

SITUATION

James, Ken, Cynthia, Robert, and Phyllis serve on a cross-functional team, the purpose of which is to survey employees to learn why retention rates are lower than the industry norm. They've finally finished compiling the survey results and have decided to celebrate by having dinner together. Just as they're about to leave work for the restaurant, Cynthia receives a call advising that her teen-age son has broken his ankle in football practice. She gives her regrets at not being able to celebrate with her team and heads home.

During the dinner, Cynthia's name comes up and the team leader, Ken, moves from a discussion of how pleasant Cynthia is to how sexy she is. Because he is out of the office, it's after working hours, and Cynthia is not present, it is perfectly acceptable for him to express his opinion.

True or False?

Court Shorts

SITUATION

Sam was the first to acknowledge the team meetings were not going as smoothly as he had hoped. The problem was, when he sat down to analyze what went wrong, he had forgotten most of what was said. At the next team meeting, he advises his team that he's planning to tape record the meeting in an attempt to understand the problem better. Because he obtained their consent beforehand, it is perfectly legal to tape record the proceedings.

True or False?

Court Shorts

SITUATION

Roberto often brings Italian pastries to team meetings—his brother owns a pastry shop. As the team gathers around the coffee and cannolis, they often make remarks such as, *"This is an offer I can't refuse."* Although he makes an important contribution to the work of the team, he has not impressed his boss as much as he has impressed his teammates. His boss fires him, with accusations that he created a "Mafia shop." The boss also explained during the termination meeting that he needed "a true American" who could deal with external customers.

Roberto sues on the basis of discrimination against national origin and will likely win.

True or False?

Court Shorts

SITUATION

Although Quentin's team is known for getting the job done, they're also known for having a good time as they do so. They often horse around with one another before the meeting starts. Joe, who provides legal counsel for the project they're implementing, is one of the most mischievous team members. He playfully dropped candy one morning in the blouse pocket of Harriette, a new addition to the team. He tapped her on the arm and told her not to worry, he wasn't planning to take the candy back. Harriette has sufficient grounds for a lawsuit.

True or False?

Court Shorts

SITUATION

Elijah is a born-again Christian who holds Bible study meetings with his team before they start their regular meetings. He had his secretary type notes from both the Bible study meetings and the regular meetings. The secretary, not part of the team, complained and Elijah was asked to stop using company resources for religious activities. He complied and even went so far as to remove all religious materials from his office.

Not long afterward, Elijah was fired for poor performance. He sued on the basis of race and religion and a violation of his Constitutional right to free speech. He will probably win the case.

True or False?

ETHICAL TEAMWORK

Information Age-ing

Approximately 10 minutes

Overview

Team leaders work hard to establish an environment that is casual, open, and relaxed. However, if that environment allows or—worse yet, encourages—age-related comments, an organization may be liable for violations of the Age Discrimination in Employment Act (ADEA). This exercise asks participants to compile a list of phrases that team members might innocently use in reference to older employees—phrases that *could* serve as the basis for subsequent lawsuits.

Purpose

To sharpen awareness of casual phrases that could lead to charges of age discrimination.

Group Size

Any number of individuals can participate. Participants will meet in small groups of four or five.

Room Arrangement

No special arrangements are required other than seating that permits easy group formation.

Materials

➤ Flipchart and marking pens
➤ Masking tape

Procedure

1. Introduce the exercise by reviewing these points:

   In Buffalo, New York, a 48-year-old salesman for a steel company was awarded nearly $1 million in damages when he claimed his dismissal was the result of age discrimination and not the result of poor work perform-

ance or even customer complaints as the company charged. Included in the evidence he offered was the fact that rising stars were often called "young tigers" by his manager.

A 64-year-old Missouri school bus driver used the phrase "old enough to retire" to help convince a jury she was discharged for age discrimination and not speeding, as the company claimed. Further proof was her supervisor's comment at her birthday party: he told her he "didn't know that she was that old." The jury awarded her $76,000 in damages.

2. Divide the class into small groups of four or five and distribute a sheet of flipchart paper and a marking pen to each.

3. Ask them to write age-related phrases such as "Young Turks" and others that, however innocent their original intention, may in fact produce subsequent legal difficulty.

4. Have a spokesperson from each group come forward and hang the list on the wall. As he or she reviews the items on the list, ask the other groups to cross off any duplicates on their own lists.

5. Continue to have each group send a spokesperson forward to review the phrases.

6. Elicit other examples of expressions or actions that could be misconstrued or—in participants' own experiences—were misconstrued and caused considerable harm. Point out that an offhand remark, a single sentence such as that spoken by Senator Trent Lott at the retirement party for Strom Thurmond, resulted in irreparable damage to Lott's career and justifiable anger among millions of American citizens.

7. Debrief with a reminder that people who work together are expected to do more than accomplish their mission. They are also expected to accomplish that mission in a safe and respectful environment.

Variation

Prepare a script ahead of time for a team leader and a team member. The script should have several phrases that could be viewed as discriminatory, such as, *"Are you thinking about retirement?"* Have two volunteers enact the script in a fishbowl setting while the remaining participants take note of the potentially dangerous comments.

Discussion

> ➤ How uncomfortable does it make you to know that simple phrases such as "You can't teach an old dog new tricks" could be used in an age-discrimination lawsuit?

> ➤ What kinds of ethical guidelines should a team leader establish at the first team meeting?

> ➤ How old do you have to be to receive protection from ADEA? (**Answer:** 40 or older.)

Quotation

"Age is a question of mind over matter. If you don't mind, it don't matter."
—LeRoy Satchel Paige

Points of Interest

With the press, in particular, and the public in general, just waiting to pounce on offensive remarks (intentional or inadvertent), today's employee must be especially diligent when interacting with others. Respectful and careful language must be employed at all times.

At the worst, offensive or inappropriate remarks can have career-threatening consequences. At best, they will make the "remarker" sound less than professional, as shown in these examples from the world of politics.

"And now, will you all stand and be recognized?"

—Gib Lewis, Texas Speaker of the House, who "welcomed" the handicapped (many of them in wheelchairs) on Disability Day

"This bill, if passed, will derail the ship of state."

—Stanley Steingut, former speaker of the New York State Assembly

"There are four departments. There's the executive, and the legislative, and the judicial, and—the Bill of Rights."

—former U.S. Senator Kenneth Wherry

"We're going to move left and right at the same time."

—Jerry Brown, former governor of California

45 Whistle-Blown in the Wind

Approximately 20 minutes

Overview

Based on real-world situations, this exercise has participants selecting one of several courses of action and discussing their selection with a partner.

Purpose

➤ To develop recognition that there are several choices possible in virtually any situation.

➤ To discuss possible courses of action to be taken when legal, moral, and/or ethical violations have occurred.

Group Size

Any number of individuals can participate. Participants will first work alone on a handout and will then discuss their answers with others who've made the same choices.

Room Arrangement

If possible, arrange table groups for four or five participants each.

Materials

➤ Projector for transparencies or for PowerPoint slides

➤ Transparency 45.1, *"Laws to Protect"*

➤ Handout 45.1, *"Whistle-Blown in the Wind"*

➤ Handout 45.2, *"Laws to Protect"*

➤ **Optional:** Token prizes of some sort for the winning team

Procedure

1. Ask participants what they know about whistle-blowing and the laws that protect those who uncover and disclose unethical or illegal practices.

2. Ask a scribe to record on a flipchart the main points of the whistle-blowing discussion.

3. Distribute Handout 45.2, *"Laws to Protect."*

4. Show Transparency 45.1, *"Laws to Protect"* and briefly discuss each law using the handout of facts provided by the Bureau of Business Practice (repeated as follows):

   NLRA (The National Labor Relations Act): Union activities are protected under this law, and employers who attempt to prevent or stop such activities are guilty of unfair labor practice. They could be taken to court for these actions.

   Title VII and ADEA (Age Discrimination in Employment Act): Workers who report discriminatory hiring questions or discriminatory statements or actions while employed are protected by these laws.

   State laws: In some states, employees who lose their jobs for reporting violations can file a lawsuit and would probably emerge victorious. Further, protections are offered in many states for those who blow the whistle on private-sector infractions.

5. Return to the flip chart and relate some of the points listed to the laws that exist to protect whistle-blowers. Correct any misconceptions that may have been stated in the step 1 discussion by alluding to the actual laws.

6. Distribute Handout 45.1, *Whistle-Blown in the Wind,"* and ask participants to work on it alone for a few minutes.

7. They will then discuss their answers with a partner. This step will take 4 or 5 minutes.

8. Arrange for further discussion by arranging subgroups as follows: those who had answers (a) and (a) will form one team. The same will be done for those with answers (a) and (b); (a) and (c); and (a) and (d). A fifth group will be composed of those who had any other combination.

9. The larger groups will continue the discussion of their choices, bringing in personal experience whenever possible.

10. Share the real-world outcome of this scenario—(a) and (b)—
    and recognize the winning team with a token prize or with
    a call to their managers, commending their insight.

11. Debrief by sharing the court's decision: They upheld the
    discharge, maintaining that foul language and disrespectful
    conduct were sufficient reasons for the firing. The whistle-
    blowing wasn't the real issue here: behavior was.

Variation

Have subgroups prepare a list of recommended steps for
employees to follow when they discover deliberate or
inadvertent wrongdoing. Make a similar list for managers to
follow once the wrongdoing is reported.

Discussion

➤ If you reported defects or unethical practices in your
  workplace, how protected would you be against retaliation?

➤ Do you think new hires should be made aware of these
  protections as part of their orientation? Explain.

➤ Have you ever been asked a question during a job interview
  that was illegal? If so, what did you do? Why did you choose
  this course of action?

Quotation

"Time is a dressmaker specializing in alterations."
—Faith Baldwin

Points of Interest

The term "boundary spanner" was coined for crisis situations
(including whistle-blowing) that affect a broad base of
stakeholders. The appointment of a spanner—who could be
inside or outside the organization—means that the values and
concerns of all potential stakeholders will be considered and
addressed. In a sense, Hans Blix and the other members of the
inspection team that investigated Iraq's nuclear weapon sites
functioned as spanners—disinterested, impartial investigators
who reported on the situation to a wide array of stakeholders.

LAWS TO PROTECT

The False Claims Act

Industry-specific laws

The Occupational Safety
and Health Act (OSHA)

The National Labor
Relations Act (NLRA)

Title VII and Age
Discrimination in
Employment Act (ADEA)

State laws

Whistle-Blown in the Wind

SCENARIO

Mark is an inspection team leader. He has been reporting defects to management for weeks now and nothing has been done. His team, which takes pride in its work and which is concerned about productivity, has been growing increasingly frustrated. Management's apparent refusal to acknowledge the problem is making the situation worse. Mark finally insisted that Nils, the quality manager, attend their team meeting, figuring there would be considerably more strength in numbers for the manager to hear.

Nils showed up and is taking a somewhat defensive stance: *"Now don't get belligerent about this,"* he placated. *"I'm sure we can work it out."*

"Forget working it out," Mark's voice rose. *"You've known about this for a month now and nothing's been done."* Mark continued, becoming more angered as he cataloged the problems and heard supporting comments from his team. He literally got "in the face" of the manager. The arguments escalated until Mark threatened to quit, emphasizing his point with profanity.

"No need to quit," Nils shouted. *"I'm firing you for insubordination."*

What do you think Nils did after the meeting? (Contemplate what you would have done.)

(a) Stood by his decision and took the necessary post-firing steps to ensure Mark was officially terminated.
(b) Offered a 3-day suspension instead of firing.
(c) Arranged a counseling session with Mark, the HR director, and himself.
(d) Asked the team as a whole for a written report of the defects problem.

What do you think Mark did? (Consider what you would have done.)

(a) Asked for a second meeting, this time with a mediator present.
(b) Go to court, claiming the firing was in retaliation for whistle-blowing.
(c) Apologize and ask to be reinstated.
(d) Ask for a transfer to a different department.

Laws to Protect

False Claims Act: Whistle-blowers may receive up to 25 percent of the amount the federal government recovers from contractors who have committed fraud against the government. The government itself is actually allowed triple damages. The use of this act is spreading to comparable situations in Medicare billing.

Industry-specific laws: Within given business arenas, laws exist to protect those who blow the whistle on companies engaged in unsafe practices.

OSHA: Under the provisions of this law, employers must create and maintain a workplace that does not jeopardize health or safety. Employees who report unsafe conditions are protected under the act.

NLRA: Union activities are protected under this law, and employers who attempt to prevent or stop such activities are guilty of unfair labor practice. They could be taken to court for these actions.

Title VII and ADEA: Workers who report discriminatory hiring questions or discriminatory statements or actions while employed are protected by these laws.

State laws: In some states, employees who lose their jobs for reporting violations can file a lawsuit and would probably emerge victorious. Further, protections are offered in many states for those who blow the whistle on private-sector infractions.

46 How Do You Spell "L-E-A-D-E-R"?

Approximately 20 minutes

Overview

More in the nature of an energizer than ethical analysis, this exercise elicits consideration of the qualities necessary for ethical team leadership.

Purpose

➤ To develop awareness of the traits possessed by ethical and effective team leaders.

➤ To evaluate the pros and cons of charisma for a team leader.

Group Size

Any number of individuals can participate in this exercise: they will work in pairs and then in quartets. (**Note:** If the total number of participants is not divisible by four, simply form small groups of three to five participants.)

Room Arrangement

No special arrangements are required.

Materials

➤ Handout 46.1, *"How Do You Spell L-E-A-D-E-R?"*
➤ Flipchart and marking pens

Procedure

1. Begin by pointing out that the topic of leadership has been explored for thousands of years. Numerous studies have been undertaken to determine exactly what qualities leaders possess. Ask for some descriptors of leaders and record them on the flipchart.

2. Post the list and start a second list by asking, "Which of these words also apply to team leaders?" After recording several, ask, "Which words not already mentioned do you feel are important for team leaders to have?"

3. Divide the group into pairs and ask each pair to select one word from either list and relate it to team leaders they've known in the past.

4. Ask each pair to join one other pair to discuss their observations.

5. Distribute Handout 46.1, *"How Do You Spell L-E-A-D-E-R?"* Ask the two-pair teams to identify the word many would associate with effective leadership—whether it's leadership of a team or any other group. (The answer is "charisma.")

6. Recognize the first team to finish by a round of applause.

7. Debrief with a discussion of the positive and aspects of charismatic leadership. The positive points are obvious and will come to participants' minds readily: the ability to develop esprit de corps, to inspire, to quicken the bonding process. The negative aspects of charisma are not thought about as often. As noted in the Points of Interest, these include an unhealthy narcissism and so intense a demeanor that few attempts at levity are made by others. The down side of charisma can also be seen in a team's tendency toward groupthink, a rush to side with the charismatic leader's viewpoint, a feeling of unease in the narcissist's presence, and an extreme desire to please the leader.

8. Conclude with a reference to the quote, which maintains that effective individuals possess both knowledge and charm— charm that is always used, ideally, toward ethical ends.

Variation

Encourage participants who actually serve as team leaders to distribute a small sheet of paper to each team member at their next team meeting. Ask each person to write anonymously a one-word answer to this question: *"What do you think is my best quality as your team leader?"* Encourage the leaders to analyze the answers after the meeting and profit from the honesty contained within.

Discussion

> ➤ What's the worst trait a team leader could possess?

> ➤ What traits do you exemplify when you lead meetings?

> ➤ In a team composed of high-powered personalities, what trait is the most important for the team leader to demonstrate?

> ➤ Think about the best teams you've ever been part of. Is there a particular quality the leaders of those teams had in common? If so, what is it?

> ➤ Think about the worst teams you've ever been part of. What quality did the meeting leaders have in common?

> ➤ Is it possible for a leader to develop a charismatic personality?

> ➤ If you believe it is possible, how do you feel about the ethics of a decision to become (more) charismatic?

> ➤ What words would you use to define the word "charisma"?

Quotation

"Besides intelligence and a knack for strategic planning, they [good managers/leaders] have enormous charm and energy. They have charisma."
—Robert Hogan

Points of Interest

Psychologist Robert Hogan of the Tulsa Institute of Behavioral Sciences has conducted research involving thousands of managers. He acknowledges there can be a dark side, though, to charisma. Basically, it's the difference between healthy and unhealthy narcissism. Among the negatives associated with destructive charismatic leaders are behaviors such as these among followers:

> ➤ A tendency to groupthink because it's safer than being a devil's advocate.

> ➤ A strong desire to please the leader, even if it means altering the truth.

> ➤ A feeling of discomfort or pressure in the presence of the unhealthy narcissist.

> ➤ Few attempts at levity.

How Do You Spell L-E-A-D-E-R?

DIRECTIONS

In each of the eight lines below, one letter of the alphabet is missing. Once you discover what it is, write it in the blank line to the right of the letters. Once you've written all eight letters in a vertical line, you'll have the trait many consider important for a team leader to possess.

1. QLXATFYMGRNUDPIWBZVSJHEKO   _____

2. XFAZBULPWCJGVNYRDEISKTQOM   _____

3. KNCOJDPEBYTUSFQZGRLVHIWMX   _____

4. IAQBFCLWJEUSKGDMXZTNOVYHP   _____

5. RLAGNBCJDPEKZMQOUVFWSXTYH   _____

6. ZAFIBTPQEJKHLCGNOUVDRWXYM   _____

7. FDSGCHOQTLUKVIXNJPYWREBZA   _____

8. ZKGLQJBYMCENOURVHSWPIEXDT   _____

ETHICAL TEAMWORK

47 Declarations of Dependence

Approximately 15 minutes

Overview

This fun exercise reminds participants of the dangers associated with a leader's decision to make overreaching, self-aggrandizing, or unkind statements.

Purpose

To highlight the damage that can be caused (to one's image as well as to the organization itself) through overly strong assertions.

Materials

➤ Transparency 47.1, *"Answers"*

➤ Handout 47.1, *"Declarations"*

➤ **Optional:** Two truth-detector awards, such as copies of mysteries or true crime stories

Group Size

Any number of individuals can participate.

Room Arrangement

A U-shaped formation works well for this exercise.

Procedure

1. Begin with a brief discussion of the importance of having a focus, a purpose, a goal—not only for a given team meeting but also for the long-term project of which a particular team meeting is just one part.

2. Tell participants you are going to distribute a list of statements (Handout 47.1, *"Declarations"*) made—or *not* made—by famous people, many of whom served in a

leadership capacity. Although we have no way of knowing whether or not they were with their teams when the statements were made, we do know that declarative statements like these can either be a source of inspiration . . . or ridicule. They can bespeak our dependence on one another as team members or they can be so embarrassing they virtually isolate us from others.

To be avoided are insulting comments and loose-cannon statements, with opinions so radical they cause the speaker to be regarded as a spokesperson for no one else but him- or herself. Not only can loose-cannon statements mislead followers, they can, on occasion, be unethical in their attempts to make it seem as if the speaker's opinion is a widely held belief.

3. Distribute Handout 47.1, *"Declarations."*

4. Ask participants to pair off and work with the person next to them. Tell them their job is to determine if the statements on the handout were truly made by the person listed beside the statement. Point out that with one possible exception, each of these individuals were in positions of power.

5. Show Transparency 47.1, *"Answers,"* containing the following correct answers to the handout questions.

   1—Yes, 2—Yes, 3—No, 4—Yes, 5—Yes, 6—Yes, 7—Yes, 8—Yes, 9—No, 10—No.

   Consider awarding a truth-detector prize to the first pair to get eight or more answers correct.

6. Conclude by asking new pairs to decide if the handout statements showed power wisely used—if only the power of attracting the press. Then, have them create a single sentence that a team leader could use to make a strong assertion about the team's purpose at the very first team meeting. The sentence should reflect strength and leadership, power, and determination—but not at the expense of team harmony. Call on each pair to share their statement and comment on the seeming use or abuse of power suggested by each.

Variation

Obtain a copy of a speech delivered by a well-known individual— the organization's CEO, for example, or the President of the United States. Analyze it for phrases that suggest power but not an unethical abuse of power. Apply the analysis to any programs dealing with Leadership, Communications, or Persuasion.

Discussion

➤ Think about the last meeting you attended. Did the meeting leader make an overarching statement that alluded to purpose or outcome and that also helped develop the sense of dependence on one another necessary for achieving that outcome?

➤ Can you think of some famous historical statements (such as Franklin Delano Roosevelt's *"The only thing we have to fear is fear itself")* that speak of a need for a collective commitment in order to survive and succeed?

➤ What statements (organizational or national) have you known to backfire—statements such as Alexander Haig's infamous *"I'm in charge here!"* asserted immediately after the shooting of President Reagan?

➤ How would you describe the statements that inspire groups? (For example, most of them are short statements.)

Quotation

"One can never consent to creep when one feels an impulse to soar."
—Helen Keller

Points of Interest

Any number of leaders (Albert Einstein, Oliver Wendell Holmes, Winston Churchill, Jack Welch) have addressed the power to be found in simplicity. That power is seen in this ethical "quick test" devised by Texas Instruments. It can be used for both actions and verbal expressions that will impact others in one way or another.

1. If you know it's wrong, don't do it.

2. If you're not sure, ask.

3. Keep asking until you are satisfied with the answer.

ANSWERS

1 — Yes
2 — Yes
3 — No
4 — Yes
5 — Yes
6 — Yes
7 — Yes
8 — Yes
9 — No
10 — No

Declarations

DIRECTIONS

Words are the team leader's best friend, for they help him or her establish purpose, keep meetings on target, and achieve intended outcomes. However, carelessly framed ideas and unkind references can do just the opposite. Your job is to determine if the person next to the quote actually spoke these words. Write **"true"** or **"false"** in the blank space in front of each to show the connection or lack of a connection) between the speaker and the spoken words.

_____ 1. "I'm just here for the drugs."—Nancy Reagan

_____ 2. "Life is indeed precious, and I believe the death penalty helps to affirm this fact."—Ed Koch, former NYC mayor

_____ 3. "Mad cow disease is a uniquely European problem and should be uniquely solved by the Europeans themselves."—General Colin Powell

_____ 4. "The reason so many people showed up at Louis B. Mayer's funeral was because they wanted to make sure he was dead."—Samuel Goldwyn

_____ 5. "Kevin Costner is like Oakland: There is no there there."—Marcello Mastroianni

_____ 6. "Bo Derek turned down the role of Helen Keller because she couldn't remember the lines."—Joan Rivers

_____ 7. "I have known many meat eaters to be far more nonviolent than vegetarians."—Mahatma Gandhi

_____ 8. "Health food may be good for the conscience, but Oreos taste a hell of a lot better."—Robert Redford

_____ 9. "There are no secret vices, especially not when it comes to gluttony."—George W. Bush

_____ 10. "Washington is the only place in the world where a person can get stabbed in the back while climbing a ladder."—Linda Tripp

ETHICAL TEAMWORK

There Is No Terror

Approximately 25 minutes

Overview

In this exercise, participants have an opportunity to learn how ethical team leaders can help drive out specific fears via specific actions.

Purpose

➤ To explore one cause of fear in the workplace.

➤ To understand better the ethical and unethical approaches to dealing with fear.

Group Size

Any number of individuals can participate. Participants will first work alone, then as an entire group, and finally in small groups.

Room Arrangement

No special arrangements are required.

Materials

➤ Flipchart and marking pens

➤ Projector for transparencies or for PowerPoint slides

➤ Transparency 48.1, *"There Is No Terror"*

Procedure

1. Begin by asking participants to think of the worst thing they have ever done, something they wouldn't want others in the group to know. (If you sense some may be uncomfortable, you can lighten the mood a bit by suggesting, "It may be the time you ate a whole chocolate cake by yourself and pretended to know nothing about its disappearance, or the time you dressed as Elvis, then drove your teenager to the

mall and identified yourself to mall-walkers as the teen's parent.")

2. After a few minutes, assure them they won't be asked to share their misdeeds but that you'd like to know how they felt when they thought they might have to.

3. To encourage input, show Transparency 48.1, *"There Is No Terror,"* and lead a brief discussion of Alfred Hitchcock's observation, *"There is no terror in the bang, only in the anticipation of it."*

4. List the tension-related feelings on a sheet of flipchart paper. (Participants will probably mention "fear," "nervousness," "shame," "guilt," "vulnerable," "worried," "shaken," "exposed," "panicked," "increased heartbeat," "anxious," "pressured." If the participant-supplied words do not number at least 10, add some of these, as you will need two words from this list to give to each small group.

5. Segue to a discussion of how these and other negative feelings (especially fear of the unknown) can impact team effectiveness if they are not resolved in some way.

6. Explain that when a team leader is just forming a group or when a leader of any kind is secretive and others don't know "where he or she is coming from," the resulting tension can seriously impact morale and output as well. Acknowledge, too, that there are individuals in positions of power who seem to play upon people's worst fears in order to advance their own agendas.

7. Extend discussion, if possible, to the question of trust, and what happens when national leaders take questionably ethical or clearly unethical actions that erode that trust. (It might, for example, be FDR's efforts to keep his disability a secret. Or, JFK's womanizing. Or, Richard Nixon's cover-up of the Watergate scandal.)

8. Assign one or two of the negative, tension-related feelings on the flipchart to each table group. Have them discuss ways a team leader can determine what the causes of these feelings might be. They should also discuss the most ethical way to deal with such feelings and the causes that produced them. For example, one cause of "anxiety" that a team member might experience could be a lack of clarity regarding the team's mission. One way to deal with this problem would be

for a team leader to state the mission on the agenda and repeatedly to assure the team that it's capable of achieving that mission.

9. Ask each group to synthesize their discussion and reduce it, if possible, to a single, memorable phrase. For example, "Agenda + Mission = Antidote for Anxiety."

10. As groups present their synthesized sentences, write them on the flipchart. Bring in the ethical relevancy of each. For example, "When groups are not clear about their mission, they may easily veer off in the wrong direction or else, completely fail to fulfill the charter they were given. Such outcomes, which can be avoided, are violations of taxpayers' or clients' trust and money (depending on the nature of the workplace make-up: government office or corporate entity)."

11. Wrap up by reviewing the group's statements on the flipchart and encouraging participants not to take advantage of co-workers who are fearful but rather to uncover those fears and reduce their causes.

Variation

Icebreaker: To help reduce the fear team members naturally bring to their first team meeting, ask each member this question and have them write down their answers: "In relation to work, what lights your fire?" Once they've finished, ask next, "In relation to work, what burns you up?" Again, have them record their answers. Go around the table and ask each person to share his or her first answer. (Allow input from others if they are so inclined.) Record the work activities that "light their fires." You can use these later when making assignments, for example, assign data analysis to the person who likes to "crunch numbers," rather than to the individual with a more creative bent.

Conclude this introductory exercise by asking each team member what bothers him or her. Make note of these answers as well, to avoid future embarrassment or transgressions. The individual who, for example, is angered when his or her integrity is questioned requires delicately posed questions. The individual who resents micromanagement will need a freer rein than others will. Respecting individuals and their unique personalities lies at the heart of ethical treatment of others.

Discussion

➤ Recall a time when someone took advantage of you by exploiting a fear you have.

➤ What is the worst error someone on your team could make?

➤ How can team leaders best handle the aftermath of mistakes team members might make?

➤ What connections can you make between fear and rumors?

Quotation

"Avoiding danger is no safer in the long run than outright exposure. Life is either a daring adventure, or nothing."
—Helen Keller

Points of Interest

Tom Peters (and numerous other experts) acknowledge mistakes as a normal part of ultimate success. Says Peters, "Mistakes are not the 'spice' of life. Mistakes are life. Mistakes are not to be tolerated. They are to be encouraged. (And, mostly, the bigger the better.)"

Team leaders can help reduce the fear of mistakes and their consequences by sharing the procedure that will be employed should a mistake be made. This is the procedure recommended by Ernest Fair:

1. Uncover causes carefully.

2. Reexamine operating procedure.

3. Apply a mistake's solution to other areas of your business.

4. Examine any recent changes in routine.

5. Remember your shortcomings.

"THERE IS NO TERROR"

"There is no terror in the bang, only in the anticipation of it."
—Alfred Hitchcock

49 This Is the House That MAC Built

Approximately 20 minutes

Overview

Through the use of puzzle pieces labeled "M," "A," or "C," participants form three groups of words (beginning with their assigned letter) that reflect or *don't* reflect ethical teamwork.

Purpose

➤ To enhance a collaborative spirit.

➤ To analyze the elements of ethical teamwork.

Group Size

Any number of individuals can participate. The group should be divided into three subgroups.

Room Arrangement

No special arrangements are required.

Materials

➤ Flipchart and marking pens

➤ Puzzle pieces

➤ **Optional:** Token prizes such as inexpensive puzzles for each subgroup member

PROCEDURE

1. Before class begins, draw a simple house on a rectangular sheet of paper (11 × 17 inches works well) and divide it into three even columns, as shown on the next page. Glue your drawing on a sheet of cardboard. (**Note:** You can choose to make your design more sophisticated—if you have artistic talent or if you wish to cut out a picture of a house and glue

it on to a large piece of cardboard. Just be sure to keep it on a rectangle and follow the same instructions.)

2. Color one column red; the next blue; and the last green. Cut the paper into three equal columns.

3. Then cut each column into 10 puzzle pieces (assuming a class of 30 participants). The pieces from the first, red column should all have the letter "M" written on the back. The pieces from the second, blue column should all have the letter "A" written on the back. Finally, the pieces from the third, green column should all have the letter "C" written on the back.

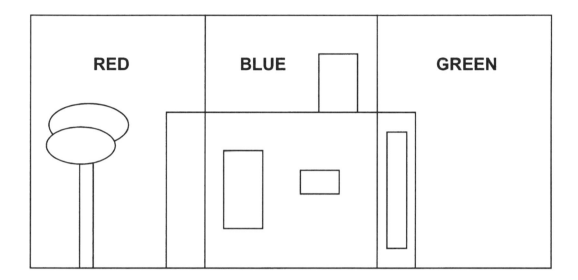

4. Distribute the pieces. Ask all those with a puzzle piece that has an "M" on the back to form one group. Ask those holding "A" pieces to form a second group, and those with "C" pieces to form a third.

5. Give all three groups this assignment: "You now have 5 minutes to list all the words you can think of that start with the letter 'M,' 'A,' or 'C'—depending on the group you are in. These words must pertain to ethical teamwork or . . . to the opposite of ethical teamwork. Examples for the 'M' group might be 'maximization (of team potential)' and, on the negative side, 'manipulation.'"

6. After 5 minutes, ask which group had the longest list. Award the token prizes, if you wish, and then ask a spokesperson to explain each of the words on the list.

7. Bring closure by asking a volunteer from each of the three teams to gather all the pieces and to complete the whole puzzle. As they do so, you can call on the other two teams to share some of their words. Once the puzzle is complete, declare, "This is the house that MAC built. Remember that, in any team effort, the sum is truly greater than any or all of the parts. The more you use the ethical 'M,' 'A,' and 'C' words we've identified, the more likely you are to achieve the results you desire."

Variation

Ask for a volunteer committee to create actual banners or single-word posters that can be mounted in meeting rooms to encourage cooperative, ethical team-building.

Encourage others to do a weekly e-mail single-paragraph newsletter (with their manager's approval). The mailing will deal with one of the positive "M," "A," or "C" words each week.

Discussion

➤ In your own experience, what is the best way to achieve harmony in a team?

➤ What unethical behaviors can lead to dysfunctional teams?

➤ Why or how do team members have a moral obligation to work together?

Quotation

"The road uphill and the road downhill are one and the same."
—Heraclitus

Points of Interest

The National Institute of Business Management, in an article titled "The Politics of Teamwork," encourages cooperation through the avoidance of "trickery, misdirection and gamesmanship." You can acquire the information you require, the Institute asserts, without being unethical. How? By being straightforward. There's a danger in assuming cooperation won't be extended, in assuming games have to be played. Find someone in the organization you trust, someone who may have information your team needs to proceed, and simply ask for what you need. Even if the individual is not in a position to share that information with you, his or her body language, pauses, and vocal intonations may give you clues that could be valuable. The Institute also recommends calling in favors when there is something your team must have in order to achieve its goal. Cooperation is, after all, built on the gives and takes, the yin and yang, the ebb and tide of relationships.

ETHICAL TEAMWORK

Story Glory

Approximately 45 minutes

Overview

Participants first take a quiz and then think of a story illustrating an ethical situation that evoked a team's respect (or lack thereof) for their team leader or their manager. The stories are then shared and voted on. One storyteller from each group regales other groups with the story.

Purpose

➤ To encourage the use of storytelling as a convincing form of communication.

➤ To use stories to illustrate ethical team-related behaviors.

Group Size

Any number of individuals can participate. Participants will first work alone and then in four small groups.

Room Arrangement

No special arrangements are required other than seating flexible enough to accommodate the formation of four small groups (up to eight plus participants in each if the class is especially large).

Materials

➤ Handout 50.1, *"Teaming by Storying Around"*

➤ Small scraps of paper—one for each participant

➤ **Optional:** A token prize such as a book of short stories for the best storyteller

Procedure

1. Begin by asking participants to think about an extremely ethical team leader (or leader of a management team) they've known in their past work experience. Then ask them to think

of a story that illustrates that person's ethical behavior. Ask them to make a note or two about the story and tell them you'll be using the stories at a later time.

2. Distribute Handout 50.1 and allow 5 to 10 minutes for participants to complete it. Then, share the answers: 1. (a), 2. (d), 3. (g).

3. Divide the class into small groups of three to five participants. Ask them to share in turn their stories regarding an ethical action taken by the leader of a workplace team.

4. Once each person has told his or her story in the small group, ask the group to decide on the story that (a) best illustrates an ethical precept and (b) was most dramatically conveyed.

5. Have the storyteller in each group whose story was voted most dramatically illustrative move to another table and share his or her story with that group. The chosen storyteller from that table will be at another table, sharing his or her story. Continue with the rotations until each of the four table groups has had a chance to hear three other stories (in addition to their own).

6. Distribute small scraps of paper and ask each person to write the name of the storyteller he or she felt had the "best" story, in terms of making an ethical point via an anecdote.

7. Ask for a volunteer to count the votes. As this is being done, bring closure to the exercise by raising the Discussion questions.

Variation
_____

Encourage the storytellers to submit their stories to publications that deal with teamwork and other management issues.

Discussion
_____

➤ At what point does persuasive ability begin to sound "slick"?

➤ What are the pros and cons associated with the use of storytelling?

➤ What stories do you use with family members to encourage ethical behavior?

➤ Can you think of organizational or national leaders who use stories to illustrate proper behavior or courses of moral action? (Jesse Jackson, for example, often speaks of his grandmother having to patch together many different pieces of fabric in order to make a quilt that kept the family warm. He uses this story to illustrate the need for various groups in our society to work together to achieve legislation that will protect the metaphorical national family.)

Quotation

"If you don't talk too good, don't talk too long."
—Ted Williams

Points of Interest

Former New York State Governor Mario Cuomo is a master of using stories as bridges to the political points he wishes to make. He also employs metaphors: the family is one he uses often to illustrate his points. So is imagery—the vision of a shining city on a hill and the impoverished underbelly of that city, for example. Study the speeches of outstanding orators and develop a new appreciation of the power of storytelling.

If you wish to join the National Storytelling Network, you can reach them at 800-525-4514.

Teaming by Storying Around

DIRECTIONS

Select the answer you believe is correct by circling the letter in front of it. Be ready to explain your answer and to provide, whenever possible, real-world examples to illustrate it or substantiate your reason for selecting it.

1. Research by J. Martin and M. Powers found that the most effective way to persuade people that a particular company was committed to avoiding layoffs was:

   (a) Telling a story.
   (b) Using statistics.
   (c) Using the story plus statistics.
   (d) Sharing a policy statement issued by the company.

2. Max DePree, former CEO of Herman Miller furniture company, asserts that every institution needs "tribal storytellers." What do you think is the purpose of such individuals?

   (a) To help ensure listening is going on.
   (b) To help retain the organization's history.
   (c) To help ensure the ongoing transference of values.
   (d) All of the above.

3. Author David Armstrong has a candy story he uses to illustrate a technique for encouraging the acceptance of change. The story involves his distributing a piece of candy to everyone at a meeting. To forestall negative comments about a change that he was proposing, Armstrong told the meeting participants, *"You are allowed one negative comment during the meeting."* After people made their comments, they had to eat their candy. Afterward, if there was no candy in front of the person, he or she was simply not permitted to attack the change being proposed. Which of the following statements associated with the above story do you feel illustrates the value of the actions that constitute this story?

   (a) Disarming can be charming.
   (b) Sometimes shock treatment is called for.
   (c) If you want people to be creative, you have to be creative.
   (d) (a) and (b)
   (e) (a) and (c)
   (f) (b) and (c)
   (g) (a), (b), and (c)

References

Armstrong, David. *Managing by Storying Around.* New York: Doubleday, 1992, pp. 135–137.

Arnold, Kristen. *Team Basics: Practical Strategies for Team Success.* Quebec: QPC Press, 2000.

Beer, Michael, and Einsenstat, Russell. "The silent killers of strategy implementation and learning." *Sloan Management Review,* Summer 2000, p. 29.

Belanger, Peter. "How to lose gracefully." *TeleProfessional,* January 1995, p. 52.

Brenner, Steven, and Molander, Carl. "Is the ethics of business changing?" *Harvard Business Review,* January–February 1997.

Bureau of Business Practice. *Leadership and the Law.* 1996, p. 27.

Carey, Robert. "The ethics challenge." *Successful Meetings,* April 1998, p. 57.

Clement Communications. "Supervisors need to know." *Supervisor's Guide to Employment Practices,* 1992, p. 1.

———. "How supervisors can tell if employees are using drugs," p. 3.

———. "Age-related 'jokes' are risky business," p. 6.

DeMars, Nan. *You Want Me To Do What?* New York: Simon and Schuster, 1997.

DePree, Max. *Leadership Is an Art.* New York: Doubleday, 1989.

"Domestic violence goes to work." *HR Manager's Legal Reporter,* pp. 1–6.

Evans, Paul. "Thrive on paradox." *Executive Excellence,* July 2000, p. 11.

Fair, Ernest. "Room for improvement." *Personal Selling Power,* September 1995, p. 68.

Farhi, Paul. "Captain without a ship." *Rochester Democrat and Chronicle,* April 30, 2001, p. 1C.

Flynn, Nancy. *The ePolicy Handbook.* AMACOM, 2001, p. 38.

Frisch, Gerald. "Internal investigation." *Successful Meetings,* May 1998, pp. 85–86.

Gardner, Howard. *Multiple Intelligences: The Theory and Practice.* New York: Basic Books, 1993.

"Good grief." *The Economist,* April 8, 1995, p. 57.

Graham, John R. "Minding your tongue." *Incentive,* May 1995, p. 80.

"Hardly a successful meeting." *Successful Meetings,* August 1992, p. 16.

Hayes, Keri. "Made in the U.S.A. (sort of . . .)." *Business Ethics,* March/April 1999, p. 6.

Kahn, Jack. "A hairy challenge." *Incentive,* December 1997, p. 12.

Krantz, Matt, and Knox, Noelle. "Some Enron board members leave other firms' rosters," *USA Today,* February 11, 2002, p. 1B.

Lawrence Ragan Communications, Inc. *Positive Leadership.* Sample Issue, p. 1.

—. "Are you guilty of giving your employees an ethical 'flea dip'?" p. 3.

Ley, D. Forbes. *The Best Seller.* Fountain Valley, CA: Sales Success Press, 1990.

Mandel, Terry. "Marketing with integrity." *Business Ethics,* September/October, 1990, p. 21.

Martin, J., and Powers, M. "Organizational stories: More vivid and persuasive than quantitative data." In: *Psychological Foundations of Organizational Behavior,* edited by B. M. Staw. Reading, MA: Scott Foresman/Addison-Wesley, 1982, pp. 161–168.

Mayer, Pam. "Profitability and the common good." *Leadership in Action,* Vol. 17, No. 3, 1997, p. 13.

McMaster, Mark, "Let the healing begin." *Successful Meetings,* October 2002, page 67.

Mescon, Michael, and Mescon, Timothy. "And then some . . ." *SKY,* August 1989, p. 92.

Michalko, Michael. *Thinkertoys.* Berkeley, CA: Ten Speed Press, 1991.

———. *Cracking Creativity.* Berkeley, CA: Ten Speed Press, 1998.

National Institute of Business Management. "The politics of teamwork." *The Politics of Executive Success,* 1988.

O'Boyle, Thomas. "Profit at any cost." *Business Ethics,* March/April 1999, pp. 13–14.

Pearson, Christine, Andersson, Lynne, and Porath, Christine. *Organizational Dynamics.* Upcoming publication of the American Management Association.

Ries, Al, and Trout, Jack. *Positioning.* New York: Warner Books, 1993, p. 78.

Roedel, Abby, et al. "101 dumbest moments in business." *Business 2.0,* April 2002, pp. 65–74.

Royko, Mike. "No mercy at hospital for grieving couple." The *Chicago Tribune.* January 25, 1995.

"The Chicago flood." *USA Today,* April 21, 1992, p. 10A.

Tracey, William R. "Managing the boss." *Solutions,* March 1995, p. 55.

Ventrella, Scott. *The Power of Positive Thinking in Business.* New York: The Free Press, 2001.

Welch, Jack. *Straight from the Gut.* New York: Warner Business Books, 2001.

Index